"*Questions that Sell* will give you the know-how to tackle your most difficult sales challenges. Reading it will take your sales conversations with customers and prospects to a whole new level of engagement. Study and devour these concepts so you gain the competitive edge over your competition. Most important, you'll solidify your existing sales relationships and win over prospects. You just have to ask the right questions. *Questions that Sell* is your tool to do so."

—RICK FARRELL, PRESIDENT, Tangent Knowledge

"*Questions that Sell* is inspirational and results-driven. It's a phenomenal resource that you can put into action immediately. Best of all, these solutions work so we can motivate our customers to take action. What really impresses me is how these questions shift us from selling products to delivering value. And that's what customers really care about. The bottom line is that *QTS* has helped us to grow our sales dramatically."

—ANDREW FIRTH, GENERAL MANAGER, ArrowQuip

"*Questions that Sell* will make us even more successful than we are today. We'll differentiate ourselves, better understand our customers, quantify the opportunities, and document the value we deliver. As a result, the sky is the limit."

—MARK BARTHEL, PRESIDENT, Springfield Electric

"I found *Questions that Sell* to be a watershed moment, revealing deep-seated personal habits that blocked my true potential. Asking the right questions allows me to put aside my agenda to be viewed as an expert and desire to be liked. The *QTS* model proves that a talking prospect is a comfortable prospect. And comfortable prospects open up to share true motivations, needs, and pains. If your challenge is compulsive talking, storytelling, and a need to prove your value, then I wholeheartedly recommend *Questions that Sell*. After 15 years of professional selling, countless training sessions, and endless coaching, I've discovered what I was missing—*Questions that Sell*."

—ADAM DUFFY, SALES EXECUTIVE, Avantik

"Listening is a skill and an art fundamental to business success. Good questions, however, are needed to shape and guide conversations. The insights Paul shares in this book improve your ability to ask more powerful, enlightening questions. Read this book. More important, apply the ideas and techniques that Paul provides."

—BILL SHULBY, GROWTH STRATEGIST AND CHANGE AGENT

"Paul Cherry's *Questions that Sell* has been a tremendous boon to me in my career. By focusing on customer needs and honing in on what motivates them, I learned to lead a conversation to a fruitful outcome through the use of targeted questions. If you find yourself doing most of the talking during a sales call, you aren't maximizing your impact and potential with the customer. Paul's techniques and formulas will show you how to get customers talking about what matters to them. With this knowledge, you can lead the conversation to the outcome you desire. Whether you are new to sales or a seasoned veteran at the top of your game, *Questions that Sell* will help you to reach the next level and continue to grow. I guarantee it."

—MAT LUCK, SALES LEADER

"It's been an amazing experience to work with Paul. *Questions that Sell* delivers great insight into our sales process and will make a huge impact moving forward."

—DARYL TODD, GENERAL MANAGER, Front Line Machinery

"As a millennial seller, *Questions that Sell* provided me with a methodology for navigating the complete sales cycle—from better prospect engagement to overcoming objections, and, most important, closing more business. It provides the framework for all sellers to incorporate the ideas into their sales style. *Questions that Sell* is a must-read—whether you're starting your career in sales or you're a senior salesperson with more than enough closed business in your pocket. *QTS* finds a way to build authentic client/customer relationships, while still continuing to grow a profitable book of business."

—JOHNATHON JONES, AUTHOR, *Embracing Adversity*

"*Questions that Sell* surprised me. I thought I was pretty good at asking questions and listening. After reading this book, I have a whole new view of the role of questions. The idea that questions are a great way to lead was one I had heard often, yet this book makes that concept real. The types of questions Paul Cherry describes—with examples and stories—build collaborative relationships, and both the questioner and the person questioned learn and benefit. *Questions that Sell* is a great reminder to me that when I think I know what's going on with another person is when it is often most important to ask. It gives me ways of doing that in a neutral fashion that bypasses my assumptions and actually gets results.

—SHEELLA MIERSON, PH.D., PRINCIPAL, Creative Learning Solutions

Questions That Sell

The Powerful Process for Discovering
What Your Customer Really Wants

Second Edition

Paul Cherry

HarperCollins
Leadership

An Imprint of HarperCollins

Questions That Sell

© 2017 Paul Cherry

Published by HarperCollins Leadership, an imprint of HarperCollins Focus LLC.

Any internet addresses, phone numbers, or company or product information printed in this book are offered as a resource and are not intended in any way to be or to imply an endorsement by HarperCollins Leadership, nor does HarperCollins Leadership vouch for the existence, content, or services of these sites, phone numbers, companies, or products beyond the life of this book.

ISBN 978-0-8144-3870-1 (TP)

Printed in the United States of America

Contents

Acknowledgments

THIS BOOK IS dedicated to my wife, Claire, who inspires and motivates me every day. To my daughters, Brooke and McKenzie, who have humbled me to balance life and work. To my mom, who has the gift to engage any stranger she meets. To my dear friend, Patrick Connor, who has been a wonderful teacher and has raised the bar for me to be my best. To David Byers, who has been an invaluable asset to growing my business. And to Michael Boyette, who has done an awesome job crafting and polishing my ideas and has played a key role in helping me write this book. A big thanks to all of you.

Preface to the Second Edition

THE ORIGINAL EDITION of *Questions That Sell* was published in 2006. In that edition, I argued that while salespeople are always facing new challenges, the fundamentals of selling are timeless.

I stand by that statement. The pace of change in business continues to accelerate. Industries have been transformed. Some have virtually disappeared. New ones have arisen. New sales roles have emerged. And yet even in the new economy, companies still need salespeople to sell their products and services.

That being said, the *environment* in which those skills are applied continues to evolve. The most profound change was already well under way when I wrote the first edition, and by now it defines selling in the twenty-first century: Everybody knows everything about everybody. Salespeople have access to much more information about buyers—and buyers have more information about salespeople and the products and services they sell. As a result, the role of the salesperson as a *provider* of information—as a walking, talking brochure—is obsolete. Your true competitive advantage is to be a *collector* of information. The only way to succeed is to know your buyer better—not just what's posted on their company website or their LinkedIn page, but their hopes, their vision, their fears—the things they reveal only to those they trust. And the only way to get that deep knowledge is by asking the right questions in the right way.

Based on the feedback I received over the years, I've completely reorganized the book and added new content. People told me that they wanted more examples of how to use questions in the field. So this edition not only shows you the key types of sales questions, how to construct them, and how to deploy them, but you'll also learn how to apply these questioning techniques in a variety of common sales situations.

I've included many new examples and templates that you can adapt to your own particular sales challenges.

I hope that this approach will make *Questions That Sell* even more useful—both for individual salespeople and as a training tool that sales managers can use with their teams.

Introduction

The world is running at a faster pace than ever before and we as salespeople must constantly adapt to new situations. In the present climate customers do not want to spend a lot of time building relationships with salespeople. They want quick and easy solutions at the cheapest price. Technological advances have forever changed our world; now that customers can do business with companies all over the globe they do not need expert salespeople. Instead, customers can get instant access to information on the Internet or from the hordes of salespeople that call them each day. Instead of trying to be the customer's friend, you as a salesperson need to cut to the chase and offer the best deal or you will lose out every time!

These statements are misguided. The idea that our world is fundamentally different from the world of 1980 or 1950, or even 1900, is ludicrous. Dale Carnegie wrote his book *How to Win Friends and Influence People* in 1938 and it is still a staple in bookstores today. We might have different technologies now than we did twenty years ago, but the people we do business with have not changed. If you do not remember anything else you read in this book, remember that. People are still people no matter what year it is.

If we look back in history we will see that every generation has believed that theirs was the one that revolutionized the world. When cars were invented, everyone assumed that life and the relationships that make it up would be changed forever. (The same is true for electricity, television, airplanes, and computers.) People believed that automobiles would cause personal relationships to disintegrate as people were free to travel hundreds of miles away from family and friends. In the end, though, the importance of real relationships has not diminished, and I contend that it never will.

How can I make such a bold statement? I have learned through years of sales and consulting that there are two types of relationships: superficial and substantive. Superficial relationships are characterized by chitchat about the weather, golf, and other neutral topics; these relationships are built on casual exchanges and they lack any real depth. An example of a superficial relationship is when you meet a client who went to the same college you did. There are a few minutes of shared memories and bonding over this coincidence, but this does not change the way you two do business. The second type of relationship is the substantive relationship, which is characterized by mutual benefit.

I ask salespeople in my seminars to describe the word *relationship*. The usual responses include descriptors such as trust, rapport, honesty, and understanding. Although these are admirable qualities to pursue with prospective clients, they are not what most clients are looking for. When customers are asked to define *relationship* in a business situation, they discuss things such as how a salesperson can bring value to their companies. The Gallup Organization conducted a major study of 250,000 sales professionals, the results of which were published in the book *Discover Your Sales Strengths: How the World's Greatest Salespeople Develop Winning Careers* by Benson Smith and Tony Rutigliano (Business Plus, 2003). They found that there was little if any correlation between having good people skills and achieving success in selling. I'm not claiming people skills are not important in selling—they are. But developing meaningful relationships takes more than being friendly. A true business relationship requires you to ascertain a customer's visions, desires, fears, and motivations. That means asking good questions—questions that engage your customers— and channeling that engagement into action.

In this kind of relationship, you as the salesperson are not solely concerned about making money or closing the deal; rather, you want to help the customer in three key ways:

1.   **Minimizing the customer's risk.** This is done by eliminating a customer's fears (about spending too much money or buying a product that will malfunction) and by making certain that the customer can hold his head up high after purchasing your product for

his company. If your customer can sleep well at night because of his dealings with you, he will definitely want to do business with you in the future.

2. **Enhancing the customer's competitive standing.** Customers, like all businesspeople, want ultimately to move ahead. If your product can make them look good in front of their colleagues and serve as a step up the corporate ladder, you will definitely earn a place at the bargaining table.

3. **Achieving the customer's goals.** A salesperson who can provide a solution that will increase profit or decrease cost is irreplaceable. If you can help a customer achieve her dream of taking her company to the next level, you will not only be a salesperson, you will be a true partner.

What do all of the above have in common? In every instance you, as the salesperson, are earning your place and achieving results in order to establish a relationship. Substantive relationships do not appear out of the blue; they are cultivated by hardworking salespeople who understand that the key to achieving success is establishing real value in the eyes of the customer.

For too many years so-called sales experts have been preaching the values of relationships without defining them. Most have argued that salespeople need only to "build rapport, honesty, and trust" in order to further their business ends. These are the characteristics of a friendship, though, and they do not necessarily build a successful sales relationship. Customers do not want to make friends; they want to see results, and substantive relationships provide those.

Do These Questions Really Work?

As a consultant, I deal mostly with salespeople who sell products and services in the business-to-business market. This means two things: The lessons I am teaching you have been tested and used by thousands of top-earning salespeople in the country. These techniques work, but they take time and effort to learn. If you are looking to create and sustain lasting business relationships with your customers in a way that sets you apart from everyone else in your industry, then you will no doubt benefit greatly from the advice I have to offer.

An excellent salesperson not only must be an expert in her field but also must be willing to embrace the role of "business shrink." What do I mean by "business shrink"? This is someone who can discover the workplace frustrations of a prospective customer. By allowing the prospective client to express his aggravations, a salesperson creates an opportunity in which the client realizes the need for change and seeks out the salesperson to provide a solution. For example, prospective clients often experience difficulties with long hours, an unusually demanding boss, or a vendor that is continually late with deliveries. A salesperson acting as a business shrink can unearth these problems by asking good questions and by listening to the answers. Once a salesperson has established her trustworthiness and willingness to listen, prospective clients will feel more at ease revealing their troubles and asking for help.

Why These Questions?

By using these techniques you can make the questions you ask prospective clients more powerful, engaging, and effective. Asking better questions will:

- **Motivate your prospective customers to do the talking.** This requires that you fight your instincts to demonstrate all of the knowledge you have about your product or industry. Instead of boring a prospective customer, get her to open up to you by asking intelligent questions and then listening to her answers. Dale Carnegie, author of *How to Win Friends and Influence People*, states that you can make a more significant impression on another person in ten minutes if you show interest in that person than if you were to spend six months talking about yourself. Asking good questions will make your prospective clients feel important.
- **Differentiate yourself from your competitors.** Studies have shown that 90 percent of seasoned sales professionals do not know how to ask good questions or are afraid to ask them. If you learn how to ask good questions, you can automatically set yourself apart from your competition.
- **Demonstrate empathy for your prospective customers.** Establishing yourself as someone who will listen to problems and frustrations will make your clients eager to talk with you. In our society,

we tend to be impatient when discussing problems: We often want to jump to the solutions. Your prospective customers, however, need first to recognize and understand their problems before they will accept their need for assistance. By creating an environment where a customer feels you understand him, you will gain access to information you would otherwise not be privy to.

- **Facilitate a prospective customer's awareness of his needs and help him come to his own conclusions.** Even if it seems clear to you, you cannot tell your prospective customer what his problems are. You need to help him go through the process of discovering for himself the problems and then he will look to you for the solution. Even those prospective customers who are aware of their problems need you to ask good questions in order to bring that pain to the surface. The frustration and other feelings that go along with the problems they have encountered will motivate your prospective customers to act, but only if you pinpoint those concerns by asking good questions.

- **Prompt a prospective customer to recognize the importance of taking action.** Once a prospective customer has uncovered her problems, she will not be hesitant to talk about possible solutions. In fact, she will be eager to discuss how you can help because she will have realized the need to rectify the situation.

- **Discover how a particular company makes a purchasing decision, as well as whom the decisionmakers are within the company.** All of the questioning techniques you are about to learn will not do you any good if you are talking to the wrong person. By asking good questions and allowing your prospective customers to talk, you will be able to find out who makes the purchasing decisions and how those decisions are made within each particular company. Without this knowledge, relationship-building techniques are useless.

- **Bring to the forefront any potential obstacles that might hinder a potential sale.** Asking good questions lets you in on the concerns of a prospective customer and his reservations about a purchase.

What Do I Expect from You?

Building real relationships takes time and energy. You should imagine your sales repertoire as a toolbox in which you already have the basics. As you learn the different question types presented in this book, you will be adding new, specialized tools to the existing set. Once you have added these tools, however, you must remember to use them correctly. If you try to remove a screw with a sledgehammer, you will not make much progress and you might ruin the wall while you are at it. Instead of jumping in with the first tool you see, take time to assess the situation and plan the best course of action. If you use the strategies in this book half-heartedly, they will not be effective; the various types of questions need to be carefully arranged and crafted for individual customers and salespeople. That time spent crafting will be recognized as well spent when you see the results of all your hard work.

I have included exercises in almost every chapter of this book. These exercises reinforce the practices I share and allow you to perfect your questioning skills before you use them. It is important that you complete these exercises, otherwise you might not be able to fully grasp the various techniques. Also, it will be difficult to digest all of the material in one sitting. I suggest that you set aside time to read each chapter and do the appropriate exercises. Then go back and read the chapter once more to ensure that you understand how and when to use that type of question. If you spend the time learning how to use my questions of engagement, I have no doubt that you will succeed beyond your expectations.

What Sorts of Problems Are Addressed in This Book?

All of the problems and hurdles you experience each day as a professional salesperson will be tackled in this book. Here are some of the most common issues that I discuss in the following chapters:

"I have trouble getting my foot in the door."
"Prospects are in a rush for information but want to wait on taking action."
"Customers say they value service but expect the lowest price."
"I feel like I am wasting too much time on opportunities that go nowhere."
"I get pushed down to deal with non-decisionmakers."
"I am ready to close the deal and then something comes up at the last minute to screw it up."

"All of the prospective customers I contact say they are not looking for new vendors, but I know they are not happy with what they have now."

"I cannot seem to get the right person."

"My presentations fall on deaf ears."

"They are always telling me they don't have the money to make a purchase right now."

What Will I Find in This Book?

At the most basic level, this book shows you how to ask questions that will get your customers talking. Salespeople are often afraid to let their customers talk. They fear that if a customer takes the conversation in the wrong direction, they will lose control and ultimately lose the sale. This could not be further from the truth. Customers have so much information they are just dying to divulge, if only we would give them the chance! When you use questions of engagement, you learn that you can control the direction of the conversation while allowing your customers to have the floor. Research has shown that during typical business interactions customers reveal only 20 percent of what is on their minds; as a salesperson who engages customers, it is your responsibility to get to the other 80 percent. Using my questioning techniques will enable you to unlock that information and use it to present your customers with tailored solutions that go beyond their expectations.

The book begins with a self-evaluation of the typical questions you should ask prospective customers. You will learn by examining those questions that many of them do not produce the desired outcome. After this exercise, you will gradually augment your repertoire with new types of questions that not only inspire conversation but also make you stand out from the crowd. All of the question types that I discuss in the book enable you to communicate better with your customers. They also serve to help build business relationships that keep your customers coming back for more.

At the heart of this book lies my belief that customers overwhelmingly respond to salespeople who express an interest in their businesses and their lives. As I say many times in the book, this does not mean that you should insist on engaging in idle small talk about sports, the weather, or other banal topics. What it does mean is that you need to cultivate real, strong relationships with your customers to make certain that their needs are met. This can happen only when you listen to your customers and really hear what they have to say. At times this might mean simply sitting there while a customer rants about your company's poor service or unreliable delivery. Other times you might have to delve into personal topics, such as a client's hopes and dreams. There could also be occasions when you will be privy to internal struggles between a customer and his boss or among various departments within a company. Although these exchanges might be exhausting, this type of business relationship can withstand corporate takeovers and changes in technology. If you are willing to put in the time and effort to cultivate genuine relationships with your customers, success will be yours.

1

A Few Questions About...Questions

SINCE THIS IS a book about questions, let's start with a few:

What, exactly, is a question? Why do we ask them? Why do we answer them? And why are they such a powerful selling tool?

I like to think of a question as a *truth-seeking missile*. And that's why a sales strategy that's built on questioning is so powerful. The best way we can create value for our customers, our companies, and ourselves is to get to the truth. Much time and money is wasted by salespeople trying to sell the wrong people the wrong solutions to the wrong problems.

As we all know, buyers don't always tell the truth. Sometimes they hold back on purpose—to be polite, to get rid of you, to gain some perceived advantage over you, or to protect themselves. More often, buyers don't tell you the truth because they don't know it. They haven't done the hard work to truly understand their own wants and needs.

We tend to take questions for granted. But if you stop and think for a moment, something very strange happens when we ask a question: *We usually get an answer.* In fact, it's hard *not* to answer a question. People even feel compelled to answer questions when it would be better to remain silent. Consider, for example, the familiar Miranda warning that we all know from police shows: Suspects actually have to be *reminded* that they don't have to answer the police's questions. Yet many do so anyway.

There's something deeply embedded in the human mind that creates a powerful compulsion to answer questions. If someone asks a reasonable question in a reasonable way, and for reasonable reasons, it's almost unthinkable to refuse to answer. It would be seen as a rude, almost antisocial act.

All human knowledge starts with questions. Nearly every profession and field of knowledge begins with a question. Detectives ask, "Whodunit?" Journalists ask, "What happened?" Science asks, "How does the world work?" Religion asks, "Why are we here?" Philosophy asks, "What is true?"

Human beings learn, grow, and succeed by exchanging knowledge with other human beings. I believe that questions are rooted so deeply in our psyche because they're the most efficient and effective tool at our disposal for acquiring knowledge. Good questions eliminate the extraneous and get to the heart of things. They allow us to acquire specific, useful, and relevant knowledge from other people. We don't have to download all of the knowledge that another person has kicking around in her brain.

But questions can do more than simply transfer knowledge from one brain to another. The best questions create *new* knowledge. The person being asked the question doesn't just tell you what he already knows. By considering the question, he discovers something—about his situation, about his values, about his wants and needs—that he hadn't understood before.

That's the transformative power of a question-based selling strategy. Good salespeople use questions to learn something about their buyers. Great salespeople use questions to help buyers learn something about *themselves*. If you can achieve that, it means you can start solving problems that other salespeople don't even know exist. Even more important, it creates a deep bond between you and your buyer. "This isn't just someone who can sell me stuff," the buyer thinks. "This is someone who helps me grow."

A Hierarchy of Questions

Much of this book is about asking deeper questions—questions that other salespeople might not think to ask, or might even be afraid to ask.

There's nothing wrong with simple, closed-end questions that a buyer can answer with a yes or no—such as, "Did you see an increase in sales last year?" Especially at the beginning of a sales relationship, you need to get some basic information. And simple questions are great for establishing rapport—they're easy for prospects to answer and don't seem threatening.

But that's where many salespeople stop. And if you don't dig any deeper, you'll never have more than a superficial relationship with your buyer. Of course, you have to earn the right to go deep with your buyer. It takes time for buyers to trust you enough to really open up. But when they do, you get to the truth. And a solution that speaks to the truth is a solution your customers will be eager to buy.

Good Questions and Bad Questions

Good questions get you closer to the truth. But some questions can lead you astray. They may create the illusion that you're making progress when at best you're going in circles. At worst, bad questions will drive buyers away. Here are some examples:

- **Leading questions.** "So wouldn't you agree that quality is the most important consideration?" "Don't you want a secure financial future?" Questions like these aren't designed to get the truth; they're designed to get agreement. We learn nothing and the customer feels manipulated.
- **Lazy questions.** "What industry are you in?" "Is this your only location?" This is information we could have gotten elsewhere, so questions like these simply waste your buyer's time.
- **Self-serving questions.** "What do you know about our company?" "Did you get a chance to look over the information I sent you?" "Are there any projects I can quote on?" "How's my pricing?" "Do you have any questions for me?" "Would you like to see a demo?" Although it's important to qualify and gauge a prospect's interest, questions like these can suggest that you are more focused on your own interests than your customer's. Like lazy questions, they can come across as product peddling or poking around for an opportunity instead of focusing on value-added solutions.
- **Trick questions.** "Which one do you want—the red one or the blue one?" "If I could show you a way to save 25 percent on your costs, would you be interested?" Buyers see these questions for what they are—a gimmick to get them to do what you want.
- **Hostile or aggressive questions.** "Didn't you have a plan in place in case of a service outage?" "Why do you continue to invest in a program that hasn't worked?" There's great value in questions that prompt a buyer to rethink old assumptions or consider new information. But questions that are designed to put buyers on the spot or make them feel stupid—especially in front of others—will prompt buyers to disclose less, not more.

A Plan for Better Sales Questions

One of the key reasons that salespeople don't ask better questions is because they lack a plan. Sales conversations can be stressful and a wrong turn can be disastrous. So salespeople often fall back on approaches that seem safe. They ask the usual sales questions in the usual way, as if they're reading them off a list. They hesitate to dig deeper, because then they don't know where the conversation will go. And they're eager to move on to the thing they know best: talking about their products or services.

If you have a plan—a set of tools—you can manage the questioning process with confidence. In the chapters that follow, we primarily focus on six types of questions that are specifically designed for sales. We'll discuss them in greater depth in the chapters that follow, but here's a quick overview:

1. Educational questions. These are questions designed to enlarge a customer's knowledge.
2. Lock-on questions. These are questions that build on what buyers have told you, which allows you to extend the conversation and dig deeper into the issues they face.
3. Impact questions. These are questions designed to explore the impact of challenges that the customer is facing.
4. Expansion questions. These are questions designed to get buyers to enlarge on what they've told you, giving you greater insight into their needs.
5. Comparison questions. These are questions that get buyers to compare one thing to another—an especially useful tool for identifying priorities and for gaining greater clarity.
6. Vision questions. These are questions that invite the buyer to see what they stand to gain, and how you can help them achieve their goals, hopes, and dreams.

Each of these question types is a powerful tool that allows you to engage your buyer on a deep level, while keeping the conversation on track and moving toward a sale. Once you master these six types, they'll become second nature and you'll know how to apply them in virtually any sales situation.

And that leads to one more question: Are you ready to start digging deeper with customers and understanding their truths? If so, let's get started.

2

Deadly Questions

Are Your Questions Costing You Business, Leaving Money on
the Table, and Putting Prospects to Sleep?

YOU PROBABLY ALREADY have a number of questions you ask your
clients during a sales call. For example:

- What do you know about our company?
- How can we help you?
- Whom are you currently working with?
- How long have you been with your current vendor?
- What do you like about them?
- What do you dislike about them?
- What's your budget?
- What are your goals?
- How much are you paying now?
- What if I could give you a better solution for a cheaper price?
  Would you be interested?
- When are you looking to make a change?
- Are you the decisionmaker?
- Can I put together a proposal for you?
- Are you ready to get started?
- May I have your business?
- How are we doing?
- Any problems?

You may feel good about a meeting during which you've asked
these questions. After all, you've garnered lots of useful information
about the buyer—what they need, what they're currently using, what

they like and don't like. You may feel you've moved the sale forward considerably. In fact, questions like these may be setting you back—because they add no value to the buyer.

There's a term for this kind of interaction: an interrogation.

Imagine yourself sitting in a small room in a police station, while a burly detective pounds you with questions. It's clear what the detective stands to gain from this exchange, but what's in it for you?

Ask too many of these types of questions and your buyers will start to feel like *they're* in that little room. They can see how *you* will benefit from these kinds of questions. But they've gained nothing for themselves. They learn nothing from your questions, because they already know the answers. So to the buyer, your questions are at best boring and at worst overbearing.

Yes, you'll eventually need to gather answers to these questions and more to make an effective recommendation to your buyer. But these are the least effective questions you can ask of a buyer because they only deliver value to you.

If your buyer is a kind and patient soul, she may politely answer all of your obviously self-serving questions, all the while hoping that at some point you're going to stop sounding like every other salesperson who's ever tried to get her business and say something valuable.

But if you don't offer any value, buyers—unlike crime suspects—possess a powerful weapon. They can end the interrogation any time they like—usually by saying something like: "I have to run to a meeting. Why don't you leave me some product literature so I can take time to digest the information and then get back to you?"

Digging Deeper

Are you a problem solver?

Of course you are. All salespeople present themselves as problem solvers.

Yet in my experience, very few salespeople ask buyers to vividly describe the problems they are experiencing. Rarely do they ask how the clients themselves are affected by those problems.

Problem-oriented questions give you, the salesperson, valuable information. But they also create value to the buyer. They invite the buyer to think more deeply about what he is trying to achieve, and what's keeping him from it. He has the opportunity to open up and vent his frustrations. And in the process, he may learn something about himself and his situation that he didn't know.

In truth, any salesperson can gather facts. But the outstanding salesperson ignites the emotions of prospective customers and uncovers what motivates them to act. Unfortunately, most salespeople *don't* know how to spur people on to action. Either they're afraid to get to the real emotions or unclear about what to do once those emotions come to the surface.

Although your usual list of questions might help you collect facts, the questioning techniques presented in the following chapters will help you go beyond mere facts and gain a deeper understanding of what your buyer needs and wants, and how you can deliver it.

Asking engaging questions will not guarantee a positive outcome. Some prospective customers will not yet be ready to admit they need help. And sometimes a buyer simply won't have a real need for your service or product. Even in these cases, engaging questions will allow you to get to the truth more quickly (or conclude it's not a good fit and move on).

So are you asking questions that dig deep? That tap into buyers' emotions and motivations? To get an honest self-appraisal of your questioning skills, let's start with two simple exercises:

Exercise 1

Take a moment to write down all of the questions you typically ask during an initial sales call to a prospective customer. List as many questions as possible.

Exercise 2

Contact a prospective client and ask some of the questions on your list. Keep track of which questions you ask, as well as how much time you spend talking during the call. Consider recording the conversation; this will help keep you honest with yourself. (Keep in mind that, depending on the state you're in, you may need the customer's permission to record the call.)

Immediately after the call ends, write up a "call report" for your own review, answering the following questions:

1. Which questions did you ask?
2. Approximately how long was the conversation?
3. What percentage of the time did you spend talking, versus your customer?
4. Did you find yourself talking more than you meant to?
5. Did your questions serve primarily your needs or the needs of your prospective customer?
6. After this call, do you have a sense of the problems your prospective client is currently facing? If so, what exactly are those problems?
7. Are you aware of the future goals of this prospective client? If so, what is her vision for the future?
8. Do you think you set yourself apart from other salespeople during this conversation? If so, state specifically how you think your questions set you apart from other salespeople in your field.
9. Are you any closer to completing the sale than you were before the call?
10. Do you have a commitment from the prospective client to pursue the next step in the sale? If so, what is it?
11. What do you think the prospective client's impression of you was after the first call?

Most likely you found several areas that you need to work on to improve your questioning techniques. That's good news—because now you've identified some areas where you can make your questioning technique better.

Inside the Buyer's Mind

Getting into the psyche of your prospective clients will allow you to ask better questions and get higher-quality information. To do this, you need to know what drives your buyer's behavior and what pushes his buttons. Here are some areas that your questions should explore:

Who is an influencer? Salespeople often talk about finding the "decisionmaker." That may even be one of the questions you ask prospects. But it's a dangerous and misguided question, and can quickly lead you down the wrong path.

Decisions—especially in complex business-to-business sales—are rarely made by one person. Organizations have safeguards to ensure that decisions aren't made until all possible factors are considered.

So asking "Who's the decisionmaker?" is based on a false assumption. Your prospective customer must report to numerous people, such as bosses, other departments within the company, colleagues on the team, stockholders, and board members, as well as customers who depend on the company to deliver a product.

What you should be looking to understand is (1) Who are all of the people *influencing* the decision to buy? (2) How much influence does each one wield? (3) What buying criteria are important to each person?

Figure 2-1 illustrates the different factors prospective customers must deal with when making a decision about whether or not to do business with you.

Who are all of these people shown in Figure 2-1? The category of "internal customers" includes bosses, board members, colleagues, and coworkers in other divisions. Internal customers set limits for how much

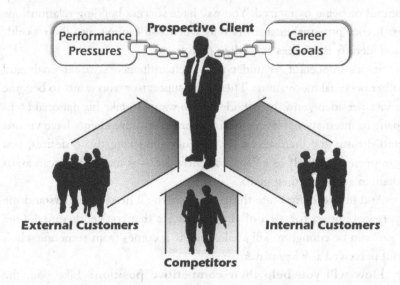

FIGURE 2-1. Factors affecting the customer's decision to buy.

money your prospective client can spend and may even erect obstacles to block the completion of a sale. Internal customers have their own agendas—agendas that you need to learn about as soon as possible in the course of the sale. Many times these agendas conflict with each other and lead to disputes among workers in the same company. If you can uncover the motivations and concerns of your prospective client's internal customers, you will be able to defuse the situation and move on with the sale.

"External customers" include those who do business with your prospective client. These are the people whom your client wants to satisfy. Therefore you should try to gain as much information about external customers as you can in order to better understand what drives your prospective customer. A prospective customer who has managerial or senior-level responsibilities will definitely be more eager to learn how your solutions could help in dealings with external customers because external customers are what keeps her in business and allows her company to grow.

What is the personal impact? Companies don't buy, people do. Just like you, your prospective customers have a personal stake in buying or not buying from you. In most cases, they're motivated to improve their standard of living, upgrade their position in the company, enhance their job security, achieve the recognition they deserve, and avoid looking stupid or being ostracized. You will have success building relationships with your potential customers only when you can get into their worlds and identify the forces at work in their lives.

So it's important to understand each influencer's career goals and other personal motivations. There's the supervisor who wants to become a vice president, and the president who wants to take his national company to international levels: All of your prospective clients have visions and dreams for themselves. By carefully unlocking those desires, you can present yourself as a "solution provider"—someone who can assist them in achieving their goals.

And just to complicate things further, you'll need to understand the personal impact for each of the influencers that you've identified. One "no" can be enough to kill a sale, even if it comes from someone who's not perceived as a key player.

How will you help their competitive position? Like you, the people you call on are worried about their competitors. Depending on the position of your prospective customers, beating the competition will be anywhere from a minor concern to their number-one priority. If you're meeting with the president of a company, it's likely to be at or near the top of the list. When discussing software with the head of information technology, however, the actions of his competitors may not even cross his mind. Either way, it is important for you as a salesperson to discover to what degree internal customers, external customers, and competitors influence the decisions of your prospective clients.

Hot-button issues. One final influence on prospective customers is the "performance pressures" they feel on the job every day. These include issues of profits, losses, and costs of production and they can dictate the day-to-day lives of many working people. A salesperson who identifies these pressures can appeal to the needs of prospective customers to meet their budgets, generate more revenues, reduce costs, save time, or reduce stress so that they can effectively meet their performance objectives.

As you can see from this list, I'm not suggesting that you need to ask more questions, but better questions. In fact, you will be asking your prospective customers fewer questions and getting more information of a higher quality. These techniques will get buyers talking about what's important to them instead of what's important to you. They will prompt the buyer to think more deeply about what he wants instead of focusing on surface-level issues such as price, features, and delivery. Equally important, they will allow you to set yourself apart from other salespeople in your field and create more meaningful, deeper relationships. Once you have finished reading this book, you will have acquired all the skills you need to craft a new set of questions, tailored to your industry and guaranteed to earn the rapport and respect of many more customers.

With all of the question types we'll be discussing, keep in mind that there's no magic formula that will unlock a sale. Your questions need to be tailored to the situation. One prospect may respond enthusiastically to one line of questioning but resist engaging with different types of questions. Some approaches will work better with decisionmakers, others with gatekeepers or administrators. Nor can you assume that, say, an engineer will be turned off by questions that get at their feelings or frustrations, or that a social worker won't care about return on investment. We hope to present you with more tools in your arsenal, so that you can try different approaches and see which ones fit.

In addition, keep in mind that you don't want your questions to come across as canned or formulaic. Prospects will be reluctant to open up to you if they sense that you're just checking off boxes on the way to the sale. Use these questions to create genuine *conversations* with buyers, not just to dress up your sales pitch.

3

Are You a Partner or a Product Peddler? The Educational Question

ONE OF THE first hurdles you face with buyers is establishing yourself as someone who can add value—not just because of what you sell, but also by virtue of who you are. High-value salespeople successfully position themselves as experts or advisers who use their expertise to improve the lives of their prospective customers.

Most salespeople sincerely want to help prospective customers by improving their business, saving them money, and expanding their share of the market.

But many prospects are cynical—and rightly so. We've all encountered too many low-value product peddlers who think their job is to show what they've got, say what it does, and ask for money.

You must work quickly to set yourself apart from that crowd, and one of the best ways is with the educational question.

Let's see how asking educational questions can help establish a high-value sales relationship. I'll use the example of a pharmaceutical sales rep because that's an especially difficult relationship to establish. Physicians are busy and their time is expensive. Moreover, they're experts in their own right and skeptical that a mere drug rep can match their own knowledge, much less tell them something they don't already know. And since reps can no longer resort to the kinds of perks and goodies that used to get them in the door, what can they do to add value? As you'll see, a well-thought question can help deliver that value, by leveraging the doctor's own expertise.

Rep: Doctor, I recently read an article on the American Academy of Pediatrics website that reported on a counseling program in Baltimore for obese children and their families. One of the biggest challenges they face is overcoming parents' denial about their children's weight issues and poor eating habits and tending to shrug off warnings from their pediatrician. I'm curious how your experience compares with that.

Doctor: Sure, we encounter that problem every week. Some families are totally out of touch when it comes to healthful eating. I just met with a mother and father who were so proud because they'd cut down their weekly fast-food meals from five to four! It's unbelievable how many children we're seeing these days with diabetes and hypertension.

What did this question do? The rep didn't tout her own expertise on childhood obesity. But the educational question positioned her in the role of consultant—someone who knows what is going on in the marketplace and in the research centers.

When asking an educational question, you not only engage the prospective customer in talk about controversial issues but also present yourself as someone with fresh information, rather than simply trying to sell your product.

The educational question is easy to compose because it requires only that you keep up with the latest news in your industry, as well as other trends or issues affecting a prospect's business—which you probably do already.

The goal in using the educational question is to *engage* your prospective customers by sharing information that's relevant to their problems. The key is to make the prospective client feel understood, and most of all understood by you. These questions are not meant to be used manipulatively; rather, they are intended to stimulate a prospect's thinking and encourage exploration of options. Once you have started a prospect thinking about different possibilities and new ways of doing business, your product will almost inevitably be seen as a solution.

A Template for Creating Educational Questions

The simplest way to create an effective educational question is to Google the industry you sell into to find news, reports, studies, and so on. You can search Google News, or simply Google something like "5-year trends in wheat farming." (If you want to do a really deep dive, check out Google Scholar, which searches academic studies and research.) Once you find some nugget of interest—ideally, an issue that people aren't yet paying attention to or something that challenges the conventional wisdom—you turn that information into a question for your buyer. For example: "I read recently in an article from _____ that _____. Tell me, how does that compare with what you are seeing?"

Here are some samples:

- "Last week I read an article in the *Wall Street Journal* that claimed drug testing is an ineffective tool to weed out poor-quality job applicants. Yet five times as many companies test for drugs today compared to ten years ago. What has been your experience on this issue?"
- "A recent article on the Business Insider website said that over 75 percent of high-tech firms today turn to foreign workers to fill web-development positions. One of the key challenges seems to be the language barrier and challenges with understanding U.S. customs and norms. Another challenge for companies is keeping up with federal laws governing foreign workers, which are in a constant state of flux. How do you manage those issues with your IT staff?"
- "In the newest issue of the *JAMA,* the editors questioned whether gene therapy is living up to its early promises. Some doctors, however, insist that breakthroughs are just around the corner. What's your view?"
- "This morning's *New York Times* quoted the Federal Reserve as saying an interest-rate hike is imminent. If it happened, how do you see this impacting your plans moving forward?"

Educational questions are great because they take advantage of something you are doing already—keeping up with industry news and trends—while elevating your status in the eyes of prospective and current customers. Do not try to pepper every conversation with educational questions: It will not appear natural. One educational question per meeting is enough to solidify your role as consultant.

Once you have asked an educational question, you will need to listen carefully to the response and tailor your follow-up questions to move the conversation in a direction where you can offer help to the prospective customer.

You should have a plan in place to transition the meeting from the educational question to the concerns of the individual with whom you are meeting. Such questions will not always lead directly into a discussion of your product or service, but a good educational question should lay the groundwork for an exchange of ideas and provoke a response from your prospective customer.

The information you use for an educational question does not necessarily need to come from a news source. As a salesperson, you interact with numerous people in your industry every day. By prefacing your question with the statement, "Some of my other clients have been telling me," you'll find that you can leverage your other customer relationships to boost your credibility with prospects. They will more fully appreciate your ability to share vital information—information that's unique to *you*, not cribbed from your company's marketing materials or a quick Google search. Prospective customers love hearing what's going on with your other customers because it shows that you're in tune with trends, industry challenges, opportunities, and how others in the industry are tackling them.

Of course, you do need to be careful about what you disclose. And that goes beyond any legal duty you have to protect confidentiality. A good rule of thumb is to ask yourself whether other customers would be upset if they were in the room listening to what you say about them. For example, I might mention a customer's name to a prospect as long as there's nothing confidential about my work with them and as long as it's not a competitor.

Even so, I tread carefully. I once put my foot in my mouth when I was describing what I'd done for another client and the prospect asked me who it was. I mentioned the company's name because they were an industry leader and thought it would impress my prospect. Not so: The prospect replied, "Oh, they have a bad reputation and their service is horrible. I guess whatever you did for them didn't help." Oh, well. You can't win 'em all.

So when that question comes up now, here's what I say: "I'm not at liberty to share the client's name. But I can discuss the issues they faced and how they overcame them." I don't recall anyone ever pushing back on that response. In fact, this response signals to prospects that you can be trusted with any sensitive information they choose to share with you.

More Examples of Educational Questions

Here are some additional examples:

- "The intense changes in technology have been especially influential on your industry. According to _____, many firms in your industry are experiencing _____. What are you experiencing?"
- "Here are three trends I'm hearing a lot about from my clients: _____, _____, and _____. Which one do you see as most important?"
- "I just attended a Webinar, which claimed, among other things, that attention spans for millennials today are 40 percent shorter than ten years ago. That would certainly have a big impact on how to hire and manage a younger workforce today. But I'm not sure I buy it. What do you think?"
- "How will you be affected by the new legislation regarding _____?"

When to Use an Educational Question

There are four key times when an educational question will be most useful:

1. As a teaser on a voice mail message so prospects will return your call
2. As an icebreaker at the beginning of a meeting
3. When a sales conversation has gotten stuck
4. When you want to add new pizazz to an existing customer relationship

As a voice mail strategy to prompt callbacks: The first instance is probably the simplest to execute. We've all experienced days almost entirely spent on the phone, leaving voice mail messages for prospective and current customers only to see none of those calls returned. It's one of the biggest frustrations when prospecting.

Rather than simply leaving your name and number (or worse, a three-minute speech about your product), leave an educational question that conveys a sense of importance or urgency, something intriguing, or something of value.

For example, consider a voice mail message left by a member of a marketing firm for an insurance executive:

Jenna: Hi, Bill. This is Jenna Matson with ABC Consulting. I was reading a report in the *Wall Street Journal* that I thought would be of interest to you. It said that increased state and federal regulations could force a number of agencies in the Southeast to either consolidate or close their doors. However, a number of firms I've spoken to want to capitalize on these changes by terminating unprofitable business and focusing their efforts on more lucrative markets. I was wondering if this is something you're dealing with. Why don't you give me a call and I can share some ideas on what other firms are doing. Thanks!

Although Bill was most likely already aware of the changes in state and federal regulations, Jenna brought those changes to the surface and presented herself as someone who could help provide some answers.

As an icebreaker: As a way to begin a conversation and build rapport with a prospective customer, an educational question not only will inspire your prospective customer to start talking but can also alleviate some of the pressure of "the sales process." The educational question doesn't immediately steer the prospective customer toward buying your product or service, nor should it be self-serving. Instead, you use the educational question to signal that you understand some of their challenges and to allow the prospective customer to voice her feelings, to vent, and to relate to you as a consultant.

Let's look at an example of the educational question used as an icebreaker:

Lucas needs to find a new way to connect with prospects. He'd asked the last one about his hobbies and was forced to sit through a twenty-minute rant about how hard it is to get tee time in the city. Eventually, the prospect looked at his watch and mumbled something about having to go to another meeting. Lucas quickly described his products as the prospect sidled toward the door.

With his next prospect, Lucas takes a different strategy. Instead of starting down in the weeds by talking about his product, he starts at the 10,000-foot level, by discussing an industry issue that will resonate with his prospect, and then glides down to a lower altitude. When you start low—which is where most salespeople start—it's hard to get your buyer to climb back up to see the big picture.

This time, Lucas starts with a research report that offers some shocking statistics about how much time employees spend on the Internet on personal business.

He refers to the report during his next meeting with Larry, the IT director of a large bank:

Lucas: Larry, I brought along a copy of a report from the Society of Human Resource Management, which shows that employees in large companies spend more than an hour each day on the Internet for personal reasons. The cost to a typical Fortune 1000 company is billions of dollars annually. I'm curious as to your thoughts about this issue.

Larry: It's interesting that you bring that up. We talked about this problem at last month's executive meeting. But we're not sure what the legalities are surrounding the issue, and we wonder how the employees would feel if we kept tabs on them. Does the report mention those issues at all?

Lucas: As a matter of fact it does . . .

Although this particular question might not lead to any business for Lucas, he has positioned himself in the IT director's mind as (1) a credible source of information and (2) someone who is attuned to the kinds of issues that are important to the company's executives. In other words, Lucas is someone he should consider when a need arises.

As a way to move a stuck conversation forward: The third way educational questions can be used is when a conversation flags and there's little or no forward momentum. Here, the goal is to get buyers to take a position and defend it, which reengages them in the conversation. And once you find out how they really feel about the subject, you can stop filling the time with idle chatter and get on with the sale. Educational questions ask prospects to stop sitting on the fence and take a side. And when they do, their emotions automatically show through.

Here is another example of an educational question, this time used to get the individual to take a position:

Kathy, who works for an employee benefits company, has been struggling through a frustrating meeting for the last thirty minutes. She has tried to get Marla, the president of a construction company, to communicate her frustrations and motivations, but Marla sits there like a stone wall.

As long as Marla plays her cards this close to the vest, Kathy's going to have a hard time connecting. So she tries to get Marla to express an opinion about something that's at least tangentially related to what she sells—in this case, employee benefits:

Kathy: As you know, attracting high-quality applicants is an ongoing struggle for many construction firms. Some of my clients insist that comprehensive health-care coverage is what employees want most. Others disagree, saying that what people want most is more take-home pay, even if the benefits are reduced. What are your thoughts?

Marla: Well, it's complicated. The rates for coverage have been increasing about 15 percent annually for the last five years, and that's a lot, especially for younger workers. But the average age of our workforce is thirty-seven and most of our guys have families. Therefore, health-care coverage is a necessity. In fact, when we've tried cheaper plans, they didn't work. Turnover increased and we found this subject coming up in our exit interviews. We discovered that talented people were leaving because our competitors offered better plans.

Kathy: Well, as you know, we work with many construction companies like yours, and we hear the same thing. We've found some creative yet competitive ways to balance costs and coverage, and they've been well received by employees.

Marla: Yes, that's something I'd like us to look into. I'll set up a meeting for you with my human resources director.

Obviously, every educational question isn't going to lead to a contract. But these questions do provide the opportunity for you to make inroads and establish yourself as a partner rather than simply someone trying to sell a product.

To reignite the spark when calling on existing relationships: Finally, an educational question is a way to create new enthusiasm with a customer you've been working with for some time. It provides a good alternative to the customary questions thrown at established customers. Instead of "checking in" or "touching base" with questions like "Is there anything I can do for you today?" or "I'll be in the area and thought I'd stop by" or "How are things going?" you can bring fresh information to the table. A provocative educational question can get a customer to revisit their emotions—the same emotions that got them to buy in the first place. And by bringing new ideas and perspectives to your clients, you lock in your position as a consultant and trusted adviser. It's a great way to keep the conversations fresh and engaging especially when you are calling on the same people again and again.

By now you may be asking yourself: Why do I need to be seen as a partner or a critical resource? How will that help me in the long run, after I have gotten the contract?

Keep in mind that if you are not *personally* adding value to the customer—and by that I mean something above and beyond the value that your product or service provides—you become expendable. If a new, cheaper product comes into town, the buyer has no reason to remain loyal. If all you are providing to your customers is a product or service, then the deciding factor when your customer is weighing a change in vendor becomes the price. Even though you might have built a relationship and had good rapport with your customer, another salesperson who can offer the same product at a 10 percent discount may easily take your place. Educational questions can help you keep from being commoditized.

A Caveat

One caveat when using educational questions: They can't be self-serving. Salespeople sometimes are tempted to use this format to try to "soften up" a hard-sell, product-focused pitch—for example, as a statement to try to establish the product's value, your company's credentials, or as lead-in to an unsolicited elevator pitch. Used in this way, educational questions will often backfire.

Educational questions need to position you as neutral and objective. Not in a deceptive or manipulative way—after all, you and your prospect both know you want to sell something—but in the sense of putting the customer's interests first. So, for example, it's best to use credible third-party information and not something like this: "We surveyed over a hundred of our customers, and 94.3% said they were extremely satisfied with our product. In fact, 4% said they would not be in business today if it wasn't for us. One customer told me yesterday that they realized a savings of over $100,000 in just one quarter. Soooo, if we could deliver results like that for you, how would you feel?" That's an "educational" question that educates no one. It doesn't lower a prospect's defenses but raises them.

Exercise

Creating effective educational questions takes some practice. You can't just mention something in the news and expect your buyer to respond. The question has to be relevant, it has to relate to what you sell in some way, and it has to lead to a meaningful conversation.

In this exercise:

1. Create three educational questions that you could use during meetings with prospective customers.
2. Formulate an educational question that can serve as an icebreaker at a meeting with someone in your industry.
3. Come up with an educational question that you can use to find out someone's opinion about a hot topic in your industry.

4

Lock-On Questions and Impact Questions

How to Uncover What Your
Buyer Won't—or Can't—Tell You

IN THE PREVIOUS chapter, we looked at how you can use educational questions to *initiate* a sales conversation, either with a prospect or with an existing customer. But how do you keep that conversation going and direct it in a way that leads to deeper insights that will unlock an opportunity? In this chapter and the ones that follow, we're going to look at several types of questions that allow you to build on what a buyer tells you. We'll focus on two types of questions to help you extend that initial conversation: "lock-on" and "impact" questions.

Have you ever faced a situation where your conversations with a buyer start off strong and then just peter out? Or a conversation where a buyer wanders all over the map but never gets you any closer to a sale? Lock-on and impact questions maintain the flow of a natural conversation while providing a way to steer the discussion in certain directions. They allow you to zero in on a particular point of interest and direct the customer's attention to that point. This saves you time and energy and helps lead you to a high-value solution for the customer.

Another benefit of these questions is their ability to clarify the thoughts and feelings of your customers. The business world is dominated by jargon. Words are often used with little or no meaning attached to them. Sometimes even the customer does not know exactly what his words mean. Often in conversation customers will use words and phrases such as *quality, strategic focus*, or *streamlining the process* without really defining them. Lock-on questions enable you to get into a customer's head to determine what she really means. Through your use of lock-on questions, you have the incredible opportunity to hear customers articulate their problems and expand on their ideas.

Dartnell Research, a leading research firm, has found that 80 percent of the time customers do not verbalize their real concerns and problems. Rather, they tend to conceal issues that might reveal vulnerability. Lock-on questions encourage customers to open up. Instead of becoming bogged down in jargon and superficiality, the conversation is rich in facts and experiences that really matter. You can then use the information to tap into the customer's emotions, beliefs, and values through the sorts of questions we'll discuss in later chapters.

How to Create Lock-On Questions

To create a lock-on question, you simply lock on to something the buyer said. But not just any old thing. You want to lock on to something that you believe could give you—as well as buyers themselves—greater insight into their needs.

Here's an example:

Customer: We have been trying to get this project off the ground for several months.

Lock-on question: I noticed you said the word *trying*. What has worked so far and what has not?

Trying is the key word to focus on in this example. The word represents feelings of frustration and discouragement at not being able to achieve a goal. Here, the customer has given you a great opportunity to bring the problems to the surface, to have her relive those feelings and then look to you for a solution. When you're looking for something to lock on to, pay attention to high-emotion words.

Let's look at some more examples.

Customer: I am looking for a partnership rather than just someone to sell me a product.

Lock-on question: Could you give me some specifics of what you mean when you say *partnership*?

Partnership is one example of business jargon that has little real meaning. As a salesperson, you might think it means your customer is looking for a win-win, where you provide real value to the customer while improving your business. But to many customers, it's simply a term to force vendors into price concessions—as in, "We want our vendors to partner with us to impact our cost structure." So it's important to lock on to these vague and often misleading terms and get customers to define them more precisely. That's the only way to discover how—or whether—you can help your buyer.

Here's another:

Customer: My company has been experiencing problems with our current vendor and we are looking for someone new.

Lock-on question: Can you give me an example of the problems you have been experiencing? [What better way for your customer to relive a painful situation created by a vendor?]

The power that comes from asking for examples cannot be overemphasized. There's a vast difference between a customer who says, "Our vendor doesn't bring anything new to the table" and one you can get to give you an example: "We were desperate for them to give us some new marketing ideas—and we would have paid a lot to get them—but instead we got a warmed-over version of last year's program." A customer who reveals a past problem experiences the emotional trauma of that problem again. He not only confides in you but also provides details of his business and his criteria for a vendor. In this example, you now know exactly what you have to do to win the business.

Lock-on questions work by providing answers that help you hone in on a certain aspect of a customer's statement. You can then either clarify the words she is using or direct the conversation according to your needs. Here are some words and phrases that can be easily used to create lock-on questions:

Trying to	Dealing with
Problems	Concerns
Hopeful	Unclear
Stressful	Seeking
Needs	Improvement

Struggling	Having difficulties
Challenges	Afraid
Frustrated	Doubts
Searching	Looking for
	Goals

These words and others like them reveal emotions and indicate that there is a problem to be solved. They signal that a customer's needs are not being completely met. When you lock on to them, you focus on the areas of concern and can begin to uncover ways to address those concerns.

Yet another example:

Customer: Our goal for this quarter is to reduce costs by 10 percent, but we have found this to be very challenging.

Lock-on question: When you say it has been challenging, what exactly do you mean?

See how simple it is once you get the hang of it? The word *challenging* connotes negative emotions and frustration owing to unattained goals. A lock-on question will help the customer vent those emotions and supply specifics that you can use to get the sale.

There are other indicators customers use that can be locked on and turned into great follow-up questions. One example is the use of the terms *we, us,* or *ours*. These pronouns tell you that there is more than one decisionmaker and more than one person affected by the problem. You can lock on to these words by asking, "I noticed you mentioned the word *we*. Who else is involved in this problem?"

Remember, when your customers give you these key words, they have opened the door for you to enter their minds. You should not feel like you are prying or being nosy. Customers want to talk about problems, frustrations, and concerns but often they do not know how to bring them up in conversation.

After identifying these words and using lock-on questions to discover the underlying problem, you can begin to present yourself as the solution provider. Your customer will be grateful that you have isolated the right problem and helped to create the solution. As was the case with the educational question, after you've used a lock-on question, you will be seen as a valuable partner in business, rather than someone who simply sells a product or provides a service.

Diagnosing Customer Problems

Lock-on questions are especially useful for diagnosing customer problems. Often, buyers are unaware of the true nature of their problems, or they're reluctant to share that knowledge with you. A customer may tell you, "We need a product that does x, y, and z." That's a conversation that goes nowhere. Either you have a product that does x, y, and z, or you don't. End of story.

A customer problem is a much richer vein to tap. Maybe your product doesn't do x, y, or z, but it's still the best solution for the problem. Maybe the buyer's problem isn't what she thinks it is. Maybe it's bigger. Or more urgent. Or more costly.

Lock-on questions allow you to quickly move the conversation in that direction. Here's an example:

Customer: We need a product that does x, y, and z.

You: Sure. May I ask why you need it?

Customer: We need to process incoming orders more quickly.

You: More quickly? Tell me more.

Customer: Well, we want to be able to deliver orders by the next day.

You: So next-day delivery isn't something you've offered in the past, but now you feel you have to? How come?

Customer: Our competitors are offering it and we have to keep up. Our sales have been down for the last two quarters and the CEO is breathing down our necks to get the numbers back up.

As you can see, a few lock-on questions have taken the conversation in a much richer direction. The customer's problem isn't finding a product that does x, y, and z. The problem or motive is how to keep up with the competition and eliminate pressure from his boss. Once you understand what the buyer's real problem is, you're in a much better position to help. And the buyer is thinking, "Wow, this person really seems to understand my situation."

When to Use Lock-On Questions

Just like the other question types introduced in this book, lock-on questions are not designed to be used continuously in a meeting. A conversation generously peppered with lock-on questions would seem false and uncomfortable to a customer and would not allow you to follow the logical progression of the meeting. Owing to their personal nature, lock-on questions should be used cautiously at the very beginning of a relationship. A customer faced with lock-on questions after just meeting you might think you are being insincere or even sarcastic. For example, if you're cold calling and get the standard "We're happy with our current vendor" brush-off, it would be presumptuous to respond, "When you say happy, what do you mean?" And used too frequently, lock-on questions can make a customer feel as if he or she is being cross-examined.

So you must understand the conditions and rules before you engage in lock-on questioning. Use lock-on questions when:

- You have a good rapport with the customer and have demonstrated empathy toward him.
- You have a sincere desire to connect with the customer.
- You respect the level of information your customer feels comfortable sharing.
- You avoid problems to which you cannot offer a solution.
- You focus on problems your competition is not addressing.
- You avoid problems that you or your company may have created in the past for this customer.

Also, if you feel lock-on questions will be viewed as too direct, you can use buffer statements to preface your question. Some examples of buffer statements include:

"Help me understand . . ."
"When you say the word . . ."
"Could you clarify for me . . ."
"What is an example that comes to mind . . ."

Exercise 1

After each customer statement, lock on to some of the words or phrases in that statement and use them to create possible lock-on questions. In the first example, I have given you a little help by putting in italics some of the words you could use to form your questions. Write as many lock-on questions you can think of.

1. "*We* have been *looking* at a few *options* to *better meet* our *needs.*"

   How many lock-on questions were you able to formulate from that simple statement? Let's hope you managed to come up with at least five or six questions for this opportunity. See "Suggested Responses" below for some ideas.

2. "Most of us agree that we should improve quality and performance while reducing overhead, all the while finding a vendor who can listen to our needs."

3. "My department has been reprimanded for not meeting our profit goals."

4. "At this time, we are struggling with a newly competitive market driven almost entirely by price."

Suggested responses:

Here are some possible responses to the first item in Exercise 1:

1. "You mentioned you were looking. For how long have you been looking?"

2. "What prompted you to start looking?"

3. "What options have you considered?"

4. "What options have you eliminated?"

5. "You mentioned *have been*. Does that mean you are still looking?"

6. "What needs are not currently being met?"

7. "For how long have your needs not been met?"

8. "What criteria are you using to determine who can best meet your needs?"

9. "Which of your needs are most important?"
10. "You mentioned *we*. Who else has input into this decision?"
11. "How will the decision to pursue a new option be made?"
12. "Let's assume your needs can be met. What do you hope to accomplish?"

By now you should be able to appreciate all of the opportunities secured when you use lock-on questions. It is important to remember, however, that lock-on questions cannot be effective if you do not listen carefully to the responses. The worst thing you can do is to get your customer to open up and reveal his emotions, and then ignore or misinterpret what he says. We all get impatient; we're all eager to move to the next step. I know I have made this mistake myself. Instead of listening, I am thinking of my next question! Lock-on questions not only force you to listen, they also take the pressure to think of another question off of you. The question will appear right in front of you—if only you listen to your customer's words.

The lock-on questioning technique is difficult for many salespeople to embrace. So many sales professionals are focused on their own agendas. They want to provide a solution without really listening to the problem. The truth is that every situation is different. Even if you are thinking, "I've heard this a dozen times before," in reality the customer has specific concerns and individual motivations that you cannot possibly know unless she tells you. Lock-on questions not only provide a tool to use in your meetings, they also force you to take the time to listen to your customers.

How to Manage a Conversation Using Lock-On Questions

Now that you have learned how to focus on a customer's emotions using the lock-on technique, you can begin to appreciate other ways it can be used. Many salespeople are wary at first about my system of questioning because they're afraid of losing control of the conversation. What they do not realize is that by asking the questions, *they* are the ones in control. The questions give you the power to direct a meaningful conversation, instead of a monologue where you simply present your product and hope the customer becomes interested.

Let's look at how good questions can guide a conversation:

Katherine sells clothing to department and discount stores, but she has been on the job for only a few months and has yet to have real success. She spent the last week calling different stores to discuss her company's clothing line and still does not have a client to call her own.

This morning, she lands a call with the vice president of purchasing for a major discount store. Katherine hopes that this potential sale will be the one to finally put her on the map. The vice president confides that the store's executives had recently held a meeting to discuss problems with their current vendor. This is the perfect moment for Katherine to use a lock-on question to uncover the exact nature of those problems. Katherine asks, "You mentioned your current vendor was not meeting your expectations. Could you give me an example of exactly what happened?"

Once the vice president starts talking, Katherine can easily find other questions to ask regarding the store's situation. She can then use this information to tailor her presentation to meet the specific needs of that store.

Katherine could assume that this is her lucky day—she's found a customer who's ready to buy. But she needs to go deeper. She needs to determine whether the store executives are committed to make a change or just blowing off steam. As all of us in business know, there are hundreds of meetings a year about changes that should be made but never are.

Instead of assuming that a company has committed to making a change, Katherine has to examine her customer's words and actions to determine where that customer is in the decisionmaking process. One of the initial ways to do this is to "qualify" the opportunity, using the techniques spelled out in Chapter 10. After qualifying, though, Katherine still needs to discover the stage of commitment in order to understand whether the company is ready to make a change in vendor, product, or service.

The Stages of Commitment

There are three stages of commitment: Should, Want To, and Have To. In the Should phase, the customer does not have the desire to change

FIGURE 4-1. Customer behaviors in three stages of commitment.

	Should	**Want To**	**Have To**
Customer behavior	The customer responds to your questions with vague answers. The customer does not recognize that she has a problem. Rather than answering your questions, she lets you talk. She is evasive when she responds to your questions.	The customer willingly shares problems and frustrations. Although the customer recognizes that there is a problem, she is not yet ready to take action to remedy the problem. Procrastination, fears, doubts or lack of confidence is blocking her from taking action.	The customer knows the benefits of change outweigh the risk of staying in the current situation. Emotions (fears, desires) are strong and so the customer is eager to take action. On average, 5% of customers are in the **Have to** phase.
Words and phrases to look for	Maybe We'll see Not right now. I'm too busy. We're satisfied.	Considering Thinking about We would like to We need to We are looking at We want to	Must Will Definitely Have to A necessity Can't afford not to
What you can do at this stage	Determine why the client lacks desire; maybe the problem is not affecting him directly. You could look for other contacts at the company or decide that the company itself is not yet open or ready to make a decision. Remember, there is not always an opportunity to be had.	**Do not** try to oversell your product/ service at this stage because you will only meet resitance. Instead, uncover the motivations. Let him verbalize them to help him see the value by getting to the **Have to** phase. One way to do this is to help him see that the benefits (ROI) outweigh the cost of his current situation.	If you encounter a customer in this phase, your timing is perfect. Let him verbalize his problems, present your solution and get a commitment. If he backs off, he was never in the **Have to** phase. Closing is not an effort because the customer will usually close himself.

and does not see the need for change. In the Want To phase, the customer wants to change and recognizes the need to change but resists taking action. In the Have To phase, the customer stands ready to make a change and will embrace a solution tailored to the company's needs. Figure 4-1 lists examples of words and behaviors of customers and their corresponding stages of commitment.

By simply listening to the words the vice president uses, Katherine can learn the level of readiness of the store's executives, and then use that knowledge to move them toward the Have To phase. She also needs to encourage the vice-president to relive the problems caused by the current vendor and explain what those problems mean for the company.

A simple way to do this is for Katherine to ask the vice president, "What have been some of the immediate effects of the problems with your current vendor?" Once Katherine brings these problems and their negative effects to the surface, she can then present herself as a sensible alternative to the current vendor. Let's look at how Katherine can use a lock-on question to achieve these goals:

Vice President: Well, this is a pretty big coincidence. We just had a meeting two days ago to discuss how our current vendors were not exactly meeting our expectations. Would you be willing to come out for a presentation?

Katherine: I'd be delighted to put together a presentation for your company, but before I do that I need to know a little more about your situation. Could you give me an example of how your current vendor hasn't met your expectations? (Lock-on question)

Vice President: Something happened just last month, as a matter of fact. We were supposed to get shipments of ten thousand bathing suits to our stores nationwide. Our supplier failed to get us the shipments on time— in fact, the swimsuits did not get to our stores for four weeks! Obviously, we expect our vendors to deliver the promised goods on time.

Katherine capitalized on a few comments made by the customer. She used a lock-on question and benefited in two ways: She found out more about the customer's business, and she succeeded in having the customer verbalize a problem with the current vendor.

The Impact Question

Once you have gotten a customer to articulate a problem and offer an example, it's time to move beyond the lock-on questions and enter a new phase: the impact question. In this phase, you will be using the information you've learned so far to get the customer to focus on the *impact* of the problem.

Everyone has problems. Some we decide we can live with, because we're not willing to invest the time, effort, and resources needed to solve them. To elevate these problems to the Have To level, begin by helping your customer quantify these problems. A customer who does not appreciate the size of the problem will not be motivated to change. The way to achieve this motivation is through the use of the impact question.

Impact questions take customers through the problem, asking them to relive it and calculate how it affects the company and themselves. The impact question often begins with coaching a customer into calculating how much money is lost by staying with the current vendor product, situation, or service.

Let's look at an example of this approach that Katherine can use with the vice president and then we will discuss the second part of impact questions.

Vice President: Something happened just last month, as a matter of fact. We were supposed to get shipments of ten thousand bathing suits to our stores nationwide. Our supplier, Shag Clothing, failed to get us the shipments on time—in fact, the swimsuits didn't arrive for four weeks!

Katherine: What effects did this delay have on your company?

Vice President: The shopping season for swimsuits is surprisingly short, so missing out on four weeks is equivalent to missing half of the season. Plus, we had empty swimsuit racks right in the front of our stores!

Katherine: How much do you charge for these swimsuits?

Vice President: About thirty dollars per suit. This year we missed half of the season. We expected to sell ten thousand swimsuits but we sold only about twenty-five hundred.

Katherine: This means that seventy-five hundred swimsuits were left in inventory and you lost approximately $225,000 in revenue. Does that seem correct?

Vice President: Yes.

Katherine: While we're at it, let me ask you something else. How much does your average customer spend when she comes into your store?

Vice President: We've found that our average customer spends $200 each time she visits our store. Owing to our wide variety of merchandise, everything from sneakers to soap, we generally have customers come in looking for one thing but ending up buying multiple items.

Katherine: Do you think it's possible that when some of your customers came in looking for swimsuits and saw the empty racks they turned around and left without buying anything else?

Vice President: Sure. According to Gartner Group, which tracks retail shopping trends, 20 percent of customers will leave if the particular product they came for is not on the shelf.

Katherine: What is your estimate of how many customers may have walked out during that four-week period when the suits were not on the racks?

Vice President: I would not be surprised if the number is somewhere around two thousand people.

Katherine: So 2,000 times $200 per person equals $400,000 of lost revenue. Would that be about right?

Vice President: Yes.

Katherine: So just this one incident cost you $625,000? How many times do you experience something like this in a given year?

Vice President: Unfortunately, with this vendor, we experience a problem like this about once a quarter.

Katherine: What would that equate to in terms of lost revenue?

Vice President [long sigh]: My guess would be about $1.8 million.

Katherine: $1.8 million per year. What does that translate to in terms of your overall revenue for the year?

Vice President: That's almost 2 percent of our revenue for the year. It's crazy to lose that because of a vendor.

As you can see, coaching your customer to quantify the problem is not simple. It requires a little patience on your part, but the effects are priceless. No doubt, Katherine's customer was well aware that his vendor was costing him business. Maybe he'd even done the math—though most customers do not recognize the extent of their problems, and it is your job, through questioning, to transform those problems into dollar signs. Either way, Katherine got her customer to *relive* that loss. How could the company *not* make a change?

It can be cathartic to help customers step back and assess a problem—especially one they've been living with for a while—and assess its true magnitude. When you take customers through this process, they become indebted to you. Unlike the case with less-skilled salespeople who skip this important step and focus only on what they're trying to sell, these conversations give buyers something important—an opportunity to vent their frustrations, and to be heard and understood. You build trust and a desire to work with you.

After the customer has quantified the problem and put a dollar value on it, you can move to the second step of the impact question. At this point, you question the customer about the impact of the problem (in this case, the problem with the vendor) on:

- The company
- The customer's position in the company
- The customer's personal well-being

You need to drive home *all* of the negative effects of the current situation until your customer almost hits rock bottom.

Impact questions get the customer to take a step back and view the entire picture. Rather than remaining wrapped up in the day-to-day issues, the customer meets the challenge of looking into the future and seeing what could happen if the current problem does not get resolved.

Here's an example of Katherine using the impact questions:

Katherine: $1.8 million per year. What does that translate to in terms of your overall revenue for the year?

Vice President: That's almost 2 percent of our revenue for the year. It's crazy to lose that because of a vendor.

Katherine: What about the time you and other personnel have to spend tracking down late deliveries? Or the overtime needed to stock shelves at the last minute?

Vice President: Last Saturday I had to spend twelve hours here working to fill empty shelves because of this problem. I had to cancel plans to watch my kid's Little League game. I was really upset and so was my son.

Katherine: That must have been frustrating. So if I could summarize this issue, what you have shared with me is a problem that is costing your company $1.8 million a year and it's costing you personally with time you could be spending with your family.

Next, Katherine uses her first impact question, targeting the effects on the *company*:

Katherine: What do you think the *impact* on your company will be if you decide to do nothing and stay with your current vendor?

Vice President: We'll probably continue to lose millions of dollars a year. That's why we can't afford *not* to change vendors. To tell you the truth, I can't believe that we have put up with this problem for so long.

Now the customer is in the Have To phase and is ready to make a change. Katherine's next impact question focuses on *the customer's role in the company*:

Katherine: What impact do you think this problem could have on you within your company?

Vice President: This is my responsibility. If we continue to lose money like this, I can't imagine I would be able to keep my job for much longer. I don't know what I would do if that happened.

What's Katherine done here? She has helped the customer recognize the problem and take ownership of it. Instead of *telling* him, she helped him realize for himself how devastating this situation is for his company and for himself.

Her next impact question focuses on the customer's personal life:

Katherine: I understand. You have a big responsibility. You also mentioned losing time with your kids. Do you think that situation will change if your problem continues?

Vice President: I don't want to keep spending late nights and weekends cleaning up the vendor's mess when I should be with my kids.

Katherine has discovered what the customer values; in this case, it is time with his family. Now she will be able to situate her product as a solution to his problem, and consequently a way for him to spend more time doing the things he wants to do and less time dealing with problems at work.

Only now—*after* she's created urgency using impact questions—is Katherine prepared to invest her time with this prospect:

Katherine: Okay, why don't we talk about the presentation?

As you can see, impact questions really emphasize the seriousness of the customer's problem. You must use your own discretion when determining how far to go with a customer. When I teach this skill to salespeople, they are often concerned about using impact questions. Many seem to believe that the questions are too personal or too controversial. In the example above, though, it is the vice president (not the salesperson) who brought up the topic of family, as well as the possibility of losing his job. Once the customer opens that door, he has invited you to discuss those topics.

Rather than shy away from tough subjects, you as the salesperson should embrace them to discover how to best help your customer. It is important to remember that as long as you are sincere in your exchange with a customer, you will both benefit. If you were to use impact questions only to scare a customer into doing business with you, that would be manipulation.

How Impact Questions Encourage Change

Most people are reluctant to change unless their situation demands it. Even when people face a problem, they usually try to just deal with it instead of looking for a way to solve it. It is often easier to avoid the pothole than to fill it. But potholes don't get smaller over time. They get bigger. So, as a salesperson, your job is to use questions to highlight a customer's problem and help your customer discover for himself the present and future magnitude of the problem.

Too many salespeople jump on their customer with a solution as soon as the customer mentions a problem. If you do this, you will be solving small problems. Instead, give the customer her time to vent. Let your customer have as much time as she wants to lament her situation. Ask questions about how the problem is impacting her job, her department, her company, and her customers. Once she has expressed all of these frustrations, she will be eager to buy from you—because now you understand her.

In most cases, customers have never taken the time to analyze their problems, nor do they calculate exactly how much a particular issue costs them. If you can take your customers through that process, so that they can figure out for themselves how much money, time, resources, and aggravation are involved in avoiding their problems, they will see how important it is to fix them.

Sample Impact Questions

Here are some questions you can use with your customers:

1. "How does this problem affect sales? Profitability? Scheduling? On-time deliveries? Quality? Production?"
2. "What do you think these problems are costing you?"
3. "How is this problem affecting the bottom line?"
4. "How much time do you spend each day dealing with this problem? If you could free up this time, what other tasks would you prefer doing?"
5. "How many employees have to address this problem? How much does it cost to train and employ these people?"

6. "When you have these difficulties, how much does it cost you to fix them?"

7. "Have you lost customers because of this problem? How much were those customers worth to you?"

8. "How is this problem affecting other areas of your business?"

9. "Let's assume you decide not to address this problem right away. What will that cost you this year?"

10. "If you do not fix this problem, what is the potential impact on your business? Can you afford to take that risk?"

11. "Can your company achieve its stated goals without addressing this problem?"

12. "Are you able to devote sufficient time to other projects while dealing with this problem?"

13. "Has company morale been affected by this problem? Have people left over this issue?"

14. "What is turnover costing you? How much does it cost to recruit and train a new employee? How long does it take before a new person can perform his job without supervision? How much does that lost time cost you?"

Once you have taken your customer through the series of impact questions and he or she has recognized the need for change, you don't want to leave him or her in the valley of despair. You need to present a brighter picture of the future. In the chapters that follow, we'll show you how to use questions to lead your buyer on that journey.

5

Opening the Floodgates:

The Power of Expansion Questions

SOME BUYERS NEED no prodding to tell you their whole life story. But most are guarded with salespeople. We've all had the experience: A sales conversation that reveals little or nothing about the buyer or his needs. Or a conversation that runs out of steam, leaving you casting about for a way to get it going again, or shifting into product-pitch mode just to fill the silence.

The more you can get buyers to reveal, the more likely you'll find a way to help them. And when buyers reveal to you things they haven't shared with any other salesperson, you gain an incredible competitive advantage. That's what expansion questions are designed to do.

Expansion Questions

The expansion question develops your basic fact-seeking request into a probing question that elicits more detailed information. It allows you to sit back and let the customer do the talking. The basic concept is to get the buyer to reveal more than simple facts. You want them to tell you a story, or reveal their thought process, or give you a peek behind the organizational curtain.

Expansion questions should begin with phrases such as:

"Describe for me . . ."
"Share with me . . ."
"Explain . . ."
"Walk me through . . ."

"Tell me . . ."

"Could you clarify something . . ."

"Can you expand upon what you just said?"

"Help me understand . . ."

These phrases signal to your prospective customers that you really want to hear what they have to say and prompt them to elaborate on their answers.

Ordinary Questions Transformed into Expansion Questions

Whenever you're about to ask a standard sales question, take a moment to consider how you can turn it into an expansion question—one that prompts the buyer to reveal more information and think more deeply. Here are some examples:

Ordinary: "Who is the decisionmaker?" "When will you make a decision?" "What is your time frame?"

Expansion: "Walk me through your company's decisionmaking process." (Here one expansion question takes the place of *three* ordinary questions.)

Ordinary: "Are you satisfied with your current system?"

Expansion: "Share with me your level of satisfaction with your current system."

Ordinary: "Is price important to you?" "Is quality important to you?" "Is service important to you?"

Expansion: "Explain to me the criteria you use to ensure you're getting the best value." (This is another situation in which three questions can be transformed into one question.)

A Sample Conversation Using Expansion Questions

Let's look at a conversation using ordinary questions and then one peppered with expansion questions.

Mark, a sales professional with ten years' experience, calls Lisa, a purchasing agent working for National Trucking Corporation. After a few pleasantries about the weather and the holiday season, Mark gets down to business:

Mark: Lisa, who is the decisionmaker at National Trucking?

Lisa: I am.

Mark: Great! So what is your time frame to make a change?

Lisa: As soon as possible.

Mark: Okay. We're ready to start whenever you are. What are your goals as a company?

Lisa: To make more money in less time.

Mark: We can definitely help you with that. Can I put together a proposal for you?

Lisa: Sure.

    Post-Game Analysis: It's doubtful Mark advanced this sale. One big reason is because he limited himself to asking ordinary sales questions. So he hasn't even scratched the surface, and he's gained no real insight into how to sell to this prospect.

A salesperson who asked expansion questions would have gotten more information and gained a better understanding of Lisa's situation. So let's see what happens when Mark uses a few expansion questions:

Mark: Lisa, I was wondering if you could walk me through your company's decisionmaking process.

Lisa: Well, I initially review any proposals dealing with a change in vendor. If I think a change is appropriate and I like what I see in the proposal, I forward my recommendation to the regional supervisor, Al. Al then looks over the information and determines whether or not a new contract would be feasible.

After Al approves the move, the next step would be to submit the proposal to our divisional vice president, John Williams. Following John's decision, the company would set up a two-week test to judge initial performance. If all goes well, the next step would be for me to create a purchase order and finalize the sale.

Mark: So, it looks like there are a lot of decisionmakers in your company. Could you share with me what specific goals you and those involved would like to accomplish if you were to make a change?

Lisa: Well, obviously our goal as a company is to make more money in less time.

Mark: Sure, but how does that translate into specific goals for, say, you, Al, and John?

Lisa: Good question. I guess we've never really come to agreement on our goals. In fact, we've been putting up with these problems for over a year now, which tells me that no one is in a real hurry to fix anything. I seem to be the only one who realizes there's a problem, because I'm the one staying late and trying to fix everything. Orders aren't processing correctly. Late shipments create logistical headaches, which I then have to solve. It takes time away from my other duties, and I'm sure things are falling through the cracks. I've brought this up to my boss several times, but I'm not getting anywhere.

Mark: Wow, it sounds like you have a real problem that no one else is paying attention to. Based on what you have shared with me, I think it would be helpful for you to introduce me to the divisional vice president. Maybe an outsider's perspective would help him see how much this problem is affecting the company, and we have a lot of experience with problems of this nature. When would be a good time for all of us to meet?

Lisa: I will find out and schedule a meeting as soon as possible.

Post-Game Analysis: By using just a few expansion questions, Mark learned a number of valuable things about Lisa and National Trucking. First, he learned that Lisa does *not* have the authority to make a final decision about changing vendors, though any change would have to be initiated by her.

Mark also discovered that Lisa is the person in the company really experiencing problems because of the current situation. Once he found this out, he knew she would be an enthusiastic promoter on his behalf because she wants the situation to be resolved.

Upon learning about the multistep decisionmaking process, Mark decided he would get Lisa's support and go directly to the top to make his pitch for a new contract. Not only did Mark garner a meeting with a divisional vice president; he gained inside information about the issue at hand and has a good understanding of how the company usually makes decisions like these.

Ordinary questions didn't give Lisa an opportunity to reveal her frustrations and negative feelings about her current situation. If Mark had simply ended the call after the first scenario, his effort would have most likely been futile. Lisa already knew her company had a problem, but she had no confidence that anyone else would recognize the need for change. What would Mark's chances for success have been in that situation? He'd prepare a standard proposal, which Lisa would forward to her boss without much enthusiasm or confidence that anyone would act on it. On the other hand, Mark's expansion questions sparked a reaction in Lisa and spurred her on to schedule a meeting with someone empowered to make a decision.

Exercise 1

Choose four or five of your questions from Exercise 1 in Chapter 2 that begin with either "who," "what," "where," "why," or "when." Then, transform those questions into expansion questions that begin with one of the following phrases: "Describe for me," "Share with me," "Explain" "Walk me through," "Tell me."

Notice that in this exercise I didn't ask you to make *all* of your questions expansion questions. Expansion questions yield a lot of insight, but they require a lot of effort on the part of the buyer. So they need to be used judiciously. You also need to include some questions that buyers can answer easily, so that they feel the conversation is moving forward.

Once you're comfortable creating your own expansion questions, you will not need to worry so much about using the exact phrases I've suggested. However, I recommend that initially you construct your expansion questions using these templates, which are designed to get customers doing the talking. Once you have embraced that concept, feel free to change the wording to better fit your style.

6

Comparison Questions:

Getting Customers to Think Sideways

DIRECT QUESTIONS—FOR EXAMPLE, asking customers to tell you what they need or want—can only get you so far. Buyers get stuck because they can only imagine one solution to their problem. Or they're not even thinking about the right problem. Or they're following a path that will lead to a dead end, when they really need to think more creatively. A question from an unexpected direction can open up new avenues for a sale, surprising both you and your buyer.

One type of question—the comparison question—is especially good at getting buyers out of a rut.

As you have probably guessed from the name, comparison questions use some variant on the word *compare*, such as *contrast, differ, as opposed to, versus,* or *from.*

Comparison questions are sophisticated and require some thought to put together. However, the benefits more than make up for the time and effort you invest. If you choose the right comparison, it can create a true "aha" moment for a buyer.

A comparison question can open up several avenues for discussion, including:

Time. Comparison questions can uncover events in the prospective customer's past, as well as what he hopes for in the future. A comparison question can also help you identify those issues that are pressing concerns, as well as how these priorities shift over months and years.

Decisionmakers. Comparison questions allow you, as the salesperson, to gain access to the inner workings of the organization and to find out who makes the big decisions. They allow you, as an outsider, to uncover competing or conflicting interests among employees of the company. You can easily find a champion (in the previous case, this would be Lisa) and identify possible pockets of resistance. Comparison questions open up the decisionmaking process and give you access to the politics within the organization. Being aware of potential political pitfalls can help you prepare a counterargument to any argument that might arise.

The Prospect's Competitors. Comparison questions can stimulate a dialogue with the prospect about the industry; they can lead to information about who is the competition, as well as what aspects of the company need improvement. Especially when you are meeting with higher-level decisionmakers, their concerns about differentiating the company's products and services in a competitive market are the same concerns you face as a salesperson. Using a comparison question can help customers see that you relate to their situation and might have a solution.

Alternative Choices. Comparison questions can open the door to new solutions for your prospective customers. You can ask questions that illuminate any dissatisfaction they feel with a current product or service and in turn show how your solution can eliminate those problems. Or you can ask questions that compare the current situation with an ideal or preferred situation.

Ordinary Questions Transformed into Comparison Questions

As with expansion questions, you can start with typical sales questions— ones you may be using already—and build on them to prompt buyers to make comparisons. Here are some examples:

Time

Ordinary: "What are your goals?"

Comparison: "Share with me what you hope to accomplish in the next twelve months. How does this compare with where you are today?" Or, "Share with me what you hope to accomplish in the next twelve months compared with where you were one year ago." Or, "Describe for me your goals three years from now." Or, "Tell me about this year's goals versus last year's."

Decisionmakers

Ordinary: "Who will make the final decision on this?"

Comparison: "Please explain to me how the decisionmaking process for this project differs from past projects you've worked on." Or, "You mentioned that Bill and Jane will both have to sign off on this project. Tell me what's important to you, as opposed to what they're looking for?" Or, "Share with me your thoughts on this approach and how it compares to what others on your team are saying."

Competitors

Ordinary: "Who are your competitors?"

Comparison: "Share with me the qualities that differentiate you from your competitors." Or, "Your customers have a lot of choices today. Tell me what you believe are the unique attributes that set you apart from others in your market."

Pains and Gains

Ordinary: "Tell me about what's not working."

Comparison: "Tell me what's working well versus what's not working so well." Or, "Compared with what you've seen in other organizations where you've worked, explain to me the gaps you see in your current organization."

Market Trends

Ordinary: "How's business?"

Comparison: "How's business this year compared with last year?" Or, "How is your business compared with others in your industry?"

Vendors

Ordinary: "What do you like about your current vendor?"

Comparison: "Describe for me the ideal qualities you look for in a vendor relationship and how that compares with your current situation." Or, "Can you prioritize what's most important to you in a vendor relationship: on-time delivery, low prices, or a wide selection?"

Similar to the benefits of expansion questions, comparison questions reveal more and prompt the prospect to do the talking. Rather than asking a question that will give you a stale answer (such as, "What's your budget?"), a comparison question actively engages the prospective customer and ensures that her answer comes with information you can use (for example, "How does this year's budget compare to last year's?"—which can open up a discussion about why the budget has or hasn't changed).

Comparison questions can also be particularly useful to home in on important buying criteria for the prospective customer. When asked whether price is important, an overwhelming majority of people will say yes. However, when asked to rank price, quality, and service, prospective customers will be forced to evaluate their priorities and verbalize what they feel most passionate about.

In the last chapter, we set out a scenario where a salesperson—Mark—used expansion questions to discover new insights about his prospect, National Trucking Company. Now let's return to Mark and see how he can build on these insights by using comparison questions.

After his first meeting with Lisa, Mark knew that this company would be a complicated sale because of the numerous personalities involved. When Lisa called him back to confirm their appointment with Vice President John Williams, Mark was prepared with some more questions about the company and its employees.

Lisa: Mark, I've set up an appointment for you and me to meet with John Williams next Friday at nine. Will that work for you?

Mark: It certainly will, and I thank you again, Lisa, for making that happen. So that we can get the most from this meeting, I want to ask you a few more questions about the company's situation, if you have the time.

Lisa: Sure, that's not a problem at all.

Mark: Thanks. I want to know if you could explain to me, as the purchasing agent, what is important to you in selecting a vendor, and how does that compare with what is important to John?

Lisa: I am always pressured to keep price low. Every quarter my region is evaluated against other regions throughout the country to see who is getting the best prices from vendors. Just last month my regional supervisor informed me that my division needs to reduce costs by 15 percent within the next twelve months. That is forcing us to choose the lowest price. But John has a different agenda. When we've been in meetings together, his focus is on increasing revenue.

Mark: Okay, that is always a tricky situation to be in because people feel as if they are being pulled in two different directions. So what would you say is most important to your company—to cut costs or to increase revenue?

Lisa: Good question. We need to focus on increasing business. Personally, I think everyone has become too focused on cost reductions, because that's seen as easier than growing revenue. Yes, it can be a quick fix, but business is about making a profit. Without a profit the company cannot survive, so that's where our main focus should be.

Mark: Thanks, Lisa. One more question. Could you describe for me what you like about your current system versus what you do not like?

Lisa: Well, the main issues I have with our current system have to do with delays. Right now, things can get backed up pretty easily and there's no mechanism to override the system and get everything out on time. These delays cost me money, and I have to stay late in order to make sure that everything is completed. Our current system saves us time when there are no complications, but otherwise it's a hassle.

Mark: Lisa, thanks so much for your time and all of your input. I look forward to our meeting with John Williams on Friday at nine.

Post-Game Analysis: Mark skillfully used comparison questions throughout this second conversation with Lisa to find out information about the company, the current system, and the personalities he would be dealing with in this sale. He can now go into the Friday meeting confident that he has a leg up on the competition because of his knowledge of the prospective customer's business, as well as the issues most pressing in the minds of Lisa and John. Lisa's willingness to share such vital information with Mark also demonstrates her desire to be an advocate and ensure that this sale will go through.

It's Friday morning, and Mark sits down in a boardroom with Lisa, his sales contact, and John Williams, vice president of National Trucking Corporation. After the requisite pleasantries, the three get down to business:

John: Mark, you come highly recommended by Lisa, so I am ready to hear what you have to say.

Mark: John, we've done a lot of work in your industry and have great results that I would like to share with you. So that I can zero in on what is most important to you, however, I would like to ask you a few questions first.

John: Fire away!

Mark: It would be very helpful if you could share with me your long-term goals and how they compare with where you were twelve months ago. (*Comparison question*)

John: My long-term goal is for this company to become the premier trucking company on the East Coast. In order to do that, we need to ensure that once a customer does business with our company, he will want to come back time and time again. Nationally, our market share has suffered because some of our competitors have been slashing their prices in order to drum up business. We are not interested in being the cheapest; however, we are interested in being the best. Twelve months ago we were relatively unknown throughout much of the Southeast, but now, thanks to an aggressive marketing campaign, we have increased our market share by three points in that region. Now we need to replicate that success nationally, while maintaining the quality we have always given our customers.

Mark: Can you walk me through the steps you are taking to make sure that your quality standards are being met? (*Expansion question*)

John: Unfortunately, we have done a poor job at taking steps to reach that goal—especially as we expand—and my concern is that we will pay the price for not planning ahead. But Lisa assures me that you will be able to help us in that area.

Mark: Well, that's right. Lisa and I talked about the problems she has been having with delays. . . .

Post-Game Analysis: Mark was able to adapt both expansion and comparison questions for this situation. He got the customer talking and positioned himself as a solution provider—someone who could help the company achieve its short- and long-term goals. All of the preparation and meetings with Lisa seem to have paid off for him.

By now you may be thinking that the key to successful sales is simply to go directly to the top: After all, the man or woman at the top is going to be the one making the final decision, right? Not necessarily. Every company is different and each person within a company holds a different portion of power. In the example of the trucking company, the vice president may have been the person to give the final go-ahead for a new contract, but the purchasing agent decides who gets the opportunity to pitch new ideas. Everyone has a role to play and your job is to understand those roles. Once you do, you can leverage the relationships and your inside information to create new business opportunities.

This is when you should remember the different influences on your prospective customer's decisions and that those influences certainly translate into both fears and motivations. While the purchasing agent felt the most pressure from her regional supervisor, the vice president was dealing with considerations about his career, as well as how his company fares against the competition. The purchasing agent's goals were more short-sighted than the vice president's because she was evaluated every quarter and the only measure being used was her ability to keep costs low. On the other hand, the vice president was viewed by the company's board of directors as a visionary—someone who would bring the company into the future. Obviously, this would not happen overnight, so he felt more flexibility when making decisions that might not show results immediately.

Understanding these differences is vital if you want to effectively communicate and ultimately do business with both of these people. Expansion questions and comparison questions allow you to probe these relationships and personalities better than ordinary sales questions would. Mark, our salesperson in the trucking example, would never have been privy to so much inside information had he not used comparison and expansion questions to engage the prospective customer and encourage her and her supervisor to do most of the talking.

Exercise 2

1. Write a comparison question that will help you uncover one of the influences affecting your prospective customer.
2. Write a comparison question that will shed light on how the prospective customer's company conducts its business.
3. Write a comparison question that addresses one of the following topics: competitors, current vendors, or current product usage.

You have learned the importance of asking good questions and engaging customers in the sales process. In this chapter, you were given two relatively simple tools to get the customer to open up and share information with you. The following chapters will provide more tools and more sophisticated questioning techniques. Remember, once you learn the basics of formulating these questions, you can adapt them to fit any sales situation.

7

Vision Questions:

Understanding Your Buyer's Hopes, Dreams, and Desires

AFTER TAKING A customer through a series of impact and lock-on questions, you will have someone in front of you who will want desperately to make a change. Vision questions enable you to show the customer a bright future, to present him with a picture of what could be if he did business with you. Whereas impact questions were all about emphasizing the negative effects of a customer's current situation, vision questions focus on the positive results that can be achieved.

At first, asking abstract questions concerning your customer's future might seem strange to you. Most salespeople are much more comfortable asking questions about the present than about the past or future. The positive effects of vision questions, however, cannot be denied. When your customer can envision a future without her current problems, a future that might include, for example, a raise, recognition, or just a life with one less problem in it, she will be your most ardent supporter.

Just like impact questions, vision questions often work best in a series, beginning with the effects a change in vendor or service provider will have on the company and then progressing to a more personal view.

These questions are very powerful because they tap into your customer's needs and desires for the future. Vision questions get people to articulate their emotions: This is what motivates people to take action. Your customers have hopes and dreams just as you do. Your job is to help them reach those dreams, which begins by getting them to articulate their goals and then mapping out the path that will take them there. The path, of course, leads through your product or service. The key is to get your customer to articulate the path, instead of jumping in and pitching the solution yourself.

The Power of "If"

Vision questions usually have the word *if* in them.

For example:

> "*If* we could eliminate that problem you are currently experiencing, that problem that is costing you [for example] $1 million per year, what would it mean to your organization? And to you?"
>
> "*If* you could implement that change, how do you think that would benefit your position and goals within the company?"
>
> "*If* you successfully implemented this change, how would it affect you personally? What would you be able to do differently?"

In particular, posing a vision question that touches on the person rather than the organization often makes salespeople uneasy. But if you are able to offer a solution that will not only help the company but also make your customer's life better, you will elevate yourself beyond the role of a typical salesperson. You will become someone who helps them achieve their goals and desires. And they will reward you not only with their business, but their trust and loyalty.

What Your Customer Needs

You might be wondering why your customers have never talked to you about their personal wants and needs, such as a desire for more time with their families or their wish for a raise. People have been conditioned in our society not to expose too much and to avoid seeming vulnerable. If another person knows what really matters to them, that person could use that knowledge to take advantage of them. So customers protect themselves by masking their real wants with superficial needs.

The best way to understand this concept is through the idea of explicit needs and implicit needs. *Explicit* needs are those needs most commonly expressed by customers when asked what they are looking for. Some examples of explicit needs include improving service or quality, growing the market share, and reducing overhead. These needs tend to be based on measurable factors such as price or percentage, but they do not go to the heart of why customers do what they do. For that, we must look at implicit needs.

Implicit needs—which are by definition unexpressed—are the driving force behind most of what we do each day, and they can be broken down into seven categories:

1.   **Success.** This is the need to feel a sense of accomplishment when you come home from a long day of work. Even if customers do not get any immediate gratification from completing a deal, that feeling of accomplishment and achievement motivates them to strive toward the goal and see the transaction through. Customers who are looking for this need to be met will often talk about wanting to "get the job done" or "earn more income" or "look for a sense of satisfaction."

2.   **Independence.** This is the need to feel some measure of *control* at work. Many of our customers have several bosses to report to, as well as shareholders breathing down their necks. When a customer can make a decision on his own, he feels in charge of his own destiny, rather than as a cog in the wheel. Customers who are looking for this need to be met will often mention yearning for "the opportunity to be creative" or "trust from my bosses to make my own decision."

3.   **Recognition.** This is the need to feel valued as a worker and to feel that your opinions matter. Even though we are paid for our work, almost all of us still look for that "pat on the back"—the signal from our boss that our efforts have been noticed. No one wants to go to work every day and feel that her voice is not heard. One sales-person told me that the worst day of her life was when she was told not to bother coming to a meeting. She realized then that her hard work was not being recognized and that she had become nearly invisible within her own company. Customers who are looking for this need to be met might discuss wanting "everyone to realize all of the hard work I do" or "people to really pay attention when I talk in board meetings."

4.   **Security.** This need is twofold: It is the need to feel that your job will not be taken away from you along with the desire to save face

and not look stupid. Although many salespeople recognize the fear their customers have of losing their jobs, most do not take into account the need of their customers to avoid embarrassment and criticism by peers and bosses. When a customer you are dealing with seems reluctant, or even procrastinates making a decision, he just may be apprehensive about making the wrong decision—or, more precisely, about being *seen* to make the wrong decision. As salespeople, we cannot give our customers any guarantees about their jobs, but we can give them the tools to show their superiors how vital they are to the company's operation. Customers who are looking for this need to be met might mention being "afraid that their job could be in jeopardy" or use key words such as *concerned, worried, unsure, afraid, troubled,* or *doubtful.*

5. **Stimulation.** This is the need to feel challenged by your job, to go to work every day and feel exhilarated instead of bored. We all have heard customers lament busy schedules and crazy deadlines, but even worse than those people are the customers who sit at their desks each day uninspired by the jobs in front of them. People enjoy using all of their faculties to solve a problem and often thrive on that situation. Customers who are looking for this need to be met will probably talk about the tasks they dislike or the everyday "fires" to put out.

6. **Peace of mind.** Buyers have a deep need to feel that their areas of responsibility are taken care of. We all devote a huge amount of unproductive time simply worrying about things we can't do much about. For example, think of a time when you were sitting home waiting for a repair person to show up. You may worry that he or she will be late, or get the date wrong, or won't be able to fix your air-conditioning, or will overcharge you, and on and on. Even though the worry doesn't really help, it's emotionally and mentally draining. When you can show buyers that they're in good hands, you lift that burden from their mind.

7. **Simplicity.** Life is complicated these days. And managing all that complexity takes time and effort. Every decision requires mental energy. The more you can make someone's life easier—for example, by simplifying their decisionmaking process, or simply by off-loading a problem they've been struggling with—the more grateful he will be.

These implicit needs will motivate your customers to do business with you, but only if you recognize those needs. Once you understand which implicit need(s) your customer wants to meet, you can use vision questions to address that need. The next exercise will ask you to determine, based on a few sentences from a customer, the implicit need *not* being met.

Exercise 1

Read the following statements from customers and then determine which implicit need the customer is trying to meet:

1. "It's tough because I have only worked here for a few months and many people still do not even know who I am. I have done some really good things since I have been here, but it does not seem like anyone has noticed."

2. "Mr. Rice, the vice president, tells me I should be concentrating on reducing overhead, but then the regional managers yell at me because they are feeling squeezed from every side. I know that if they all just let me do my job, I would be able to find a good solution. Instead, it seems like everyone wants me to do things his way and then nothing gets done."

3. "Every day it's the same thing. First, I get all of the calculations from the previous day and then I summarize them for the marketing department. I could be doing this in my sleep."

4. "For the last few months things have really sucked. Every deal I brokered fell through. I just want to see one sale through from beginning to end. Is that too much to ask?"

5. "This vendor has really screwed us over. They've been late with deliveries, and sometimes when we get the merchandise it's damaged and we have to send it back. Over the last eighteen months, that's happened four times! I don't want to get blamed for all of the lost revenue, but I'm afraid that's exactly what will happen."

How to Use Vision Questions

Once you have determined which of your customer's needs is not being met, you can use that information to tailor vision questions for him. Let's go back to Chapter 4, which discussed impact questions, for an example. The vice president of a chain of department stores said, "If we continue to lose money like this, I can't imagine I would be able to keep my job for much longer. I don't know what I would do if that happened." It is obvious from this statement that the vice president needs to feel a greater sense of security. Now that you are aware of this fact, you can use it to create a vision question just for him.

Vision Questions for a Customer Seeking Security

"If you and I could find a solution to this problem, what effect do you think that would have on the company in the next five years?" *(It would help ensure our financial success, and therefore my job.)*

"If you came to your boss with a solution that would save the company nearly $2 million per year, what would that mean to you?" *(It would show my boss that I'm proactive and valuable.)*

"If we're successful with this program, how do you think your life would look five years from now?" *(Maybe I'd be making a lot more money.)*

As you can see, vision questions are not overly complicated. They simply ask the customer to look to the future and imagine how great a change could be. Once you have gotten a customer to the point at which you will use a vision question, you have earned the right to convince her how your product or service can help achieve that goal.

Let us use the examples from Exercise 1 in this chapter to practice creating this type of question.

Exercise 2

After reading the examples, formulate a series of vision questions specific to the customer's implicit need. The first one has been done for you (see "Answer").

1. "I'm fairly new to this plant and starting to get to know some of the people here. I've implemented some changes but my boss doesn't seem to take notice."

2. "I'm pulled in so many directions, I can't even think straight. If everyone would just let me do my job!"
3. "I'm putting out the same old fires. Nothing changes. I'd rather spend my time with my customers."
4. "Every one of the last ten quotes have fallen through. What's it going to take to win some business?"
5. "My boss is on me to reduce the turnover in this department. Otherwise, I may be the next guy to go."

Answer

Answers to statement 1:

"In our discussion we have calculated that using the new assembly line could save the company $1 million over the next two years. What impact would that have on your company?"

"If you were able to save the company $1 million and pave the way for a new plant in Phoenix, how do you think you would be perceived at your company? What would it mean to you personally?"

Other Uses for Vision Questions

Vision questions do more than serve as the second half of impact questions. They can be used by themselves when it seems that a customer has already come to the Have To stage of commitment and does not need to be convinced with impact questions.

Vision questions can also be a way to salvage a conversation in which impact questions were not as effective as they should have been.

Furthermore, generalized vision questions can be used during other parts of a meeting to determine the motivations of a customer. Sometimes customers are not as free in expressing their frustrations and concerns as those in the above exercises. A customer who seems standoffish and aloof might open up if asked a vision question.

Let's take an example. Our salesperson, Jeff, has been meeting for an excruciatingly long hour with Sandra, a prospective customer. Although Jeff has used educational questions, expansion questions, and lock-on questions, Sandra has yet to really open up and engage Jeff in conversation. Jeff is ready to throw in the towel and call it a day because he feels like he has not gotten anywhere with this sale, but he decides to ask one more question before he leaves.

Jeff: Sandra, I realize you're very busy. Let me ask you a question. Imagine yourself three years from today and you are looking back to today. What will make you happy knowing that you accomplished something during this time frame?

Sandra: In three years I really hope to have moved up from divisional manager to vice president.

Jeff: What steps do you think you will need to take in order to move up to that position?

Sandra: Well, I have excellent performance reviews as well as four years' experience as a divisional manager, but I need to find a way to really make a dent in the bottom line.

Jeff: As you know, I have gathered data from your people and done extensive research into how we could save you money. Based on that data, I know that my service could earn you almost $3 million a year in licensing fees. If you were to bring that kind of revenue to your superiors, how would that help you attain your three-year goal?

Sandra: Hmmm, that's an interesting proposition. I was not aware that the opportunity was that large. If what you are saying is correct, I would be stupid not to present this idea. Let's see if I can arrange a meeting with the president next Tuesday morning. Is there any chance you could be there?

Some More Vision Questions

Here are some additional ways to ask vision questions, which you can use as a template for your sales conversations:

"If you were able to achieve your goal, in what ways would it benefit the organization? How would it benefit your department? How would it benefit you personally?"

"What is your vision for the future of your company [department, team, territory]? What do you see as the key steps you will need to take in order to get you there?"

"What is your dream for the future of your career? What will you have to accomplish in order to get where you want to be?"

"Try to picture yourself a year from now. Share with me exactly what has to happen in order for you to be satisfied with the outcome."

"What could you stop doing if this problem were solved? And what would you do with that free time?"

"If you could accomplish this objective, what would that mean to you?"

"If this problem were solved, what would it enable you to do?"

There are no downsides to using vision questions because of the positive tone and upbeat message they present. On a typical day, most of the working population remains locked in the present and does not think about the future and what it might bring for them. If you can use vision questions to lift your customers out of the present and into a sunny future, they will be forever grateful to you, not to mention the fact that they will almost certainly want to do business with you.

8

Putting It All Together:

From Prospect to Close

I HAVE GIVEN you a lot of information, and it might be difficult to imagine what a sales call looks like when it incorporates all of the tools presented in this book. Unfortunately, I cannot be there with you to demonstrate these techniques, so I've chosen to do the next best thing.

On the following pages you will find a complete scenario of a sales call, from beginning to end and using all of the different types of questions I have introduced. I've used an example from the medical field, because salespeople are often viewed with suspicion in this field, and it can be especially tough to break into this world and establish your credibility.

If you don't do business in this area, don't worry. I have left out much of the technical jargon in order to focus on the ways in which salespeople can connect with customers. And the basic challenges are similar in other fields, especially technical or specialized markets where "laypeople" have a hard time getting taken seriously.

As you read the following example, take note of the various methods employed by the salesperson and the perseverance needed to complete this sale.

Samantha, Our Salesperson

Samantha sells to hospitals and other patient-care facilities. Her product, the MedInfo app, gives doctors and nurses instant access to a patient's medical history through their smartphones, tablets, and computers. It helps hospitals coordinate patient care, improve scheduling of procedures, and reduce duplication of tests. As a result, health systems can run more efficiently, and reduce error rates by as much as 10 percent.

Whereas previous systems were slow and cumbersome to use, the MedInfo interface is quick and intuitive. In addition, it helps protect patient privacy by eliminating paper records, which can be read by anyone with access to a hospital room. The MedInfo app is password protected, ensuring that only authorized personnel can view confidential information.

There are several problems Samantha must overcome in order to complete any sale. One of her biggest problems is the product's complexity. Though the interface is simple, the hospital's IT department has to do a lot of work on the back end to connect all of the information. In addition, the app has multiple "power user" features that give clinicians and hospitals powerful insights into patient care. But these features take time to explain, and Samantha finds that most customers tune out.

Another problem Samantha must face involves the initial expense of her product. The cost to set up the MedInfo app in an average-size hospital often exceeds $300,000. This money is needed to create a secure computer network that will be accessible throughout the hospital, to meet federal privacy regulations, and to configure the app to work with the hospital's existing systems.

Most low-level administrators or purchasing agents react with horror when they hear prices like this, but Samantha must convince them of the benefits of her system in order to reach the real decisionmakers. Once Samantha can illustrate the positive aspects of her product to hospital executives, most can see the potential value of the app and agree that the costs are reasonable. But hospitals are highly bureaucratic, and getting past these low-level people is the hardest part of the sale.

Day 1. Samantha Talks with a Manager in Accounting

Today Samantha calls on Greenville Hospital, a medium-size hospital in the suburbs of a large city. Samantha knows that this hospital has been trying to revamp its image and grow its market share, but it has come up against a wall because of the larger-than-life reputations of other nearby hospitals. She hopes that employees of the hospital will view her product as a great opportunity rather than as just another expense.

Samantha first calls on a manager in the accounting department who is listed on the hospital's website as a contact. Here's their conversation:

Samantha: Good morning, Richard.

Manager: Yes, how can I help you?

Samantha: I'm calling to talk with you about a product used by state-of-the-art hospitals around the world. The product is MedInfo app. Have you heard of it?

Manager: No, I haven't. What is it?

Samantha: It's an app that gives doctors and nurses instant access to a patient's medical history through their smartphones, tablets, and computers.

Manager: That sounds interesting, but I bet it is expensive.

Now Samantha needs to qualify the situation to find out how interested the manager might be.

Samantha: I know that we all worry about price, but there are times when the benefits outweigh the cost. So that I can better understand your situation, may I ask you just a few questions?

Manager: Yes, please go ahead.

Samantha: When the hospital considers a new IT-related product, what is the typical evaluation process?

Manager: Well, right now the hospital is not evaluating or approving *any* new purchases. Over the last three or four years we have seen increasingly smaller profits and so the powers that be have proclaimed a moratorium on spending. We just can't do it.

Samantha: Well, thanks so much for your time. I really appreciate it.

What has Samantha learned? The most important information *isn't* that the hospital has declared a moratorium on new purchases. If the value proposition is right, organizations can find the funds. But Samantha realizes from her qualifying question that this accounting manager is taking direction from "the powers that be" and doesn't have the power to make a purchasing decision at this time. Furthermore, he probably does not have all that much insight into the day-to-day operations at the hospital.

Samantha decides not to spend her time with midlevel administrators like Richard because they have been intimidated into cutting their spending. Instead, she will focus on the doctors and nurses—the people who would actually be using her product—and hope that they will have enough influence to make the hospital executives listen.

Samantha calls the hospital directory and asks for the name and phone number of the head nurse. She calls the number but she gets sent directly to voice mail. Knowing that the head nurse probably sifts through dozens of calls each day, Samantha tries her best to be memorable with her message:

> "Hi, Karin. My name is Samantha Fox, with MedInfo, and I am calling about the fact that nurses spend half their time on administrative functions—time they could better spend on patient care. We've helped over twenty-five thousand nurses reduce their workload on average 40 percent, and I'd like to discuss with you how our product could make your life a little easier. If you could call me back when you get a chance, we could discuss this further. My number is 555-555-1212. Thanks!"

Although Samantha left only a short message, she piqued Karin's interest. Karin wondered, "Is there really something out there that could make my life less stressful? I hope so!" Though she's skeptical of Samantha's claims, she decides it's worth at least a phone call. She makes a note to call Samantha back first thing the next morning.

Day 2. Samantha Talks with the Head Nurse

At nine the next morning, Samantha gets a call from Karin. Unlike the accounting manager she spoke with the day before, Samantha thinks that Karin will not be as focused on budgets and cutting spending. Samantha has learned from her past selling experiences that head nurses are concerned about keeping their nurses happy (internal customers) and making sure that the patients are safe (external customers). If she can steer the conversation toward these two areas, Samantha believes she will make an ally in Karin. Here's their conversation:

Samantha: Karin, thanks so much for returning my call. As I mentioned yesterday on your voice mail, our company, MedInfo, has empowered more than twenty-five thousand nurses to do what they love doing—providing outstanding patient care, rather than pushing mounds of paperwork. I don't know if what we offer is suitable for your needs but, to find out, may I ask you some questions?

Karin: Yes, go right ahead.

Samantha: Many nursing professionals we work with say they spend more than 50 percent of their time on paperwork and record-keeping, a problem that was recently highlighted in *Nursing* magazine. Did you happen to see the article? And is this an issue that you face? [*That's a great educational question to get the conversation started.*]

Karin: I didn't see the article. But I'd have to agree that our nurses probably spend half of our time on record-keeping. It's a ridiculous waste of time! [*Samantha can tell she hit a hot button by the way the customer responds to the question. Once that happens, the salesperson immediately begins to build rapport with the customer because the customer wants to open up and vent her frustrations.*]

Samantha: With all of this time spent on records, how does that affect the care given to patients? [*This is a great question that follows up on the customer's statements.*]

Karin: That's the issue. I know my nurses are great at their jobs and extremely dedicated to our patients, but it seems that over the past several years we have become stretched too thin. When I first became a nurse, fifteen years ago, it was typical for a nurse to be responsible for six patients at a time. Now my nurses must care for twelve patients each, and we have more paperwork than ever before! The insurance companies and the new privacy laws mean that each patient has a stack of paperwork traveling with him—paperwork that the nurses have to fill out. My nurses are exhausted and frustrated.

Samantha: It sounds like hiring and retention could be an issue. I know that the national rate for turnover in nursing is pretty high. How is it for Greenville? [*Once again our salesperson just follows the flow of the conversation and asks questions related to topics brought up by the customer.*]

Karin: Well, the national average is 15 percent, but for the last two years we've had a 20 percent turnover rate. It is really unfortunate because we have lost some great nurses owing to these long hours and hectic schedules. [*Our salesperson has uncovered one motivation for the customer: keeping internal customers—in this case nurses—happy.*]

Samantha: When you lose good nurses, is it hard to find replacements?

Karin: Sure it is. There is a nationwide nursing shortage right now, and even when we find new nurses we have to spend several weeks training them. This means that another nurse must take time out from caring for her patients and train this new person.

Samantha: How much of that training involves paperwork and record-keeping?

Karin: Good question. I'd have to say at least 20 percent. Our systems are hard to work with.

Samantha: And how does this training affect patients? [*Here our salesperson is broaching the topic of external customers.*]

Karin: My nurses are extremely good at what they do and they give the patients the best care possible. When they're stretched this thin, however, the best is not always good enough. It's hard not to feel responsible. As head nurse, I am supposed to be the manager and the motivator, but lately I have found it difficult to stay positive. [*It's evident that this customer needs something to turn her situation around. It is now finally time for our salesperson to talk about her product.*]

Samantha: Well, Karin, you know there are no magic bullets. I do have something, however, that I think could help. My product is MedInfo. It's an app that gives doctors and nurses instant access to a patient's medical history through their smartphones, tablets, and computers. It's highly intuitive and really streamlines record-keeping.

Karin: Sounds interesting, but how would it help me?

Samantha: The app has been shown to reduce the time nurses spend on paperwork by 40 percent on average. When a nurse administers medication, for example, instead of having to write down the date, time, type of medication, and amount on a patient's chart, she simply presses a few buttons and it is automatically recorded in the patient's record. Within each hospital, the MedInfo app uses a secure network and server so that all charts are automatically up to date. This eliminates the risk of a patient getting a double dose of medication, the wrong dose, or not getting his medication at all. The app also offers instant up-to-date reference material about drug interactions and correct dosage for specific heights and weights. And there's a program that allows you to enter a patient's symptoms and view a list of possible medical and nursing diagnoses. Somerville Hospital has been using this technology for the past year and has witnessed dramatic improvements in patient care.

Karin: Wow! You are working with Somerville? They have a great reputation in our region. I'm not sure I totally understand the app, but it sounds like it could save my nurses a lot of time *and* improve patient safety. You know what? I'd really like for you to talk to the doctor's committee about this. They will be meeting tomorrow at noon. Sorry for the short notice, but if I could set it up, would you be able to come in?

Samantha: I'd love to. What do you think they would be most interested in hearing about? [*Samantha wants to make sure that she can tailor her information to the specific group with which she is meeting. She also wants to make sure she gets as much inside information as possible about these other decisionmakers.*]

Karin: I think that the doctors would be especially interested in the special functions you talked about—specifically getting the latest information on drug interactions and treatments. Also, most doctors would embrace a system that would help them reduce their paperwork burden. And another thing, doctors in our hospital also worry about malpractice lawsuits because insurance premiums have gotten so high. Anything that would better insulate them from lawsuits would be a definite plus. [*Our salesperson has discovered that these customers focus on external customers as well as personal career goals.*]

Samantha: Well, thanks so much, Karin. I'll see you tomorrow.

Day 3. Samantha Meets with the Doctor's Committee

Samantha arrives early for the noon doctor's meeting in the hospital lounge. Although Karin couldn't be at the meeting because of a prior commitment, she gave Samantha permission to share any of the comments and concerns she voiced the day before.

After a few pleasantries are exchanged and a brief introduction and overview of her company, Samantha begins.

Samantha: I want to thank all of you for agreeing to meet with me. So that I can be respectful of your time and address what's important to you, could you share with me your level of satisfaction with the current patient chart system at Greenville?

Doctor #1: I would say we're not all that satisfied. Currently we use a combination of computer and paper files, and information from one system often doesn't seem to make it to the other system. And personally, I hate filling out all of this paperwork because it seems to be redundant and a waste of time. As doctors I think we would all rather be spending more time with the patients, rather than filling out paperwork in triplicate.

There are murmurs of agreement from the other doctors.

Doctor #2: Plus, I'm afraid that a fatal mistake is going to be made one day. You have so many different people—doctors and nurses, not to mention orderlies—who interact with the patient and I worry that communication breaks down. If I prescribe a medication and tell one nurse, she might be busy and hand it off to another nurse. That is fine and it happens all the time, but what if the second nurse didn't hear the instructions correctly and gives the wrong medication or the wrong dosage? I don't want to be liable for that.

The doctors all nod their heads.

Samantha: So, if I am hearing you correctly, you want less paperwork to fill out and a better system of communication with other hospital personnel. That's what our app is designed to do.

Samantha goes on to tell the doctors about the MedInfo app and reiterates the benefits she'd explained to Karin. The doctors are excited about the possibilities of this new system. The doctor in charge contacts the hospital president's secretary, who schedules an appointment for Samantha in two days.

Day 4. Samantha Gathers Information and Researches Issues Relevant to Greenville Hospital

The day before her big meeting with the president of Greenville Hospital, Samantha is convinced that her product could really help this hospital, its staff, and its patients. She knows that the MedInfo app could help put Greenville on a par with the other major hospitals in the area, such as Somerville.

In order to be fully prepared to meet the president, Samantha organizes all of the information she learned from the nurses, doctors, and even the manager of accounting. She catalogs some of the facts and figures she has discovered:

- The nursing staff at the hospital has a 20 percent turnover rate—5 percent higher than the national average.
- There are five hundred nurses on staff at the hospital, which means that each year Greenville is losing one hundred nurses. According to Karin, this is due in large part to the extreme stress and high level of frustration because of disorganization and miscommunication.
- It costs at least $10,000 to recruit and hire a new nurse.
- The doctors fear that miscommunication and poor documentation might lead to more malpractice suits. The hospital is already involved in three lengthy and costly suits and cannot afford any more.
- The medical error rate at Greenville Hospital, according to public records, is 4 percent, which translates to 20,000 errors per year. (The hospital sees 500,000 patients per year.)
- Greenville Hospital has one of the lowest insurance reimbursement percentages of any hospital in the country. The Insurance Institute, which keeps records on insurance reimbursement, tells Samantha that Greenville receives payment for only 73 percent of its bills because of poor record-keeping. Most hospitals nationwide average at least 85 percent reimbursement, and some get as high as 90 percent.

After Samantha talks with Karin and the doctors, she goes back to her friend in accounting. She asks him to estimate how much money each year has to be written off because of improper record-keeping. He estimates the loss to be close to $5 million each year.

Day 5. Samantha Sits Down with the President of the Hospital

Samantha knows that she cannot hold back when talking with Diane, the president of the hospital. The MedInfo app could save Greenville Hospital millions of dollars each year and improve patient care. All Samantha has to do now is convince Diane that an initial investment of $400,000 is well worth it.

Samantha knows that at the CEO level, most prospects are chiefly concerned with taking the organization to the next level, beating the competition, and reducing costs.

After several minutes of small talk, Samantha gets down to business. She shares with Diane all of the information she has learned over the last week, including the worries of doctors and nurses about patients and the large amount of money lost every year owing to poor record-keeping. Diane is impressed with Samantha's ability to gather information and lay it all out on the table.

After hearing Samantha's assessment of the hospital's condition, Diane shares her own frustrations. She wants to make changes but fears that others in the hospital (such as the doctors and nurses) will resist change. Samantha's information tells her that she and her staff actually share many of the same concerns, and that the hospital is ripe for an overhaul.

Samantha then gives Diane a chance to envision what the future could bring for her and the hospital if all of these problems were solved.

Samantha: If we could eliminate these problems of miscommunication and disorganized record-keeping—problems that are costing you at least $4 million each year—what effects do you think that would have on Greenville? [*This vision question can help the customer focus her attention on the benefits of the product to the organization as a whole.*]

Diane: If we could do that, the hospital would have the cash to acquire new medical technologies and recruit superstar doctors rather than trying to simply make payroll each month.

Samantha: If you could go to the hospital's board of directors and tell them that you have saved the hospital $4 million each year and increased the hospital's standing in the community, what would that mean to you? [*This second vision question emphasizes the effects of this change on the customer, rather than the organization.*]

Diane: I'd be less worried about being replaced by some cutthroat businessperson who was concerned only about money. I am a physician, and practiced medicine for twenty years before taking an administrative position. I know that a hospital can't excel without great physicians and nurses, but the board of directors has been pressuring me to get rid of some of our best staff because of their high salaries. If I can go to them and show them that we will be saving millions of dollars, I think we'll all feel a little more secure in our jobs. [*This answer reveals the customer's fear of losing her job and her fear of failure because she is also at risk of losing her staff.*]

Samantha: Diane, that is great to hear. In your role, it's important to keep your eye on the big picture. Let's say three years from now, what professional goals would you want to have achieved by then?

Diane: Well, I want to worry less about the hospital's budget, and concentrate more on attracting the most innovative doctors and purchasing the best medical technology that money can buy. In fact, I want Greenville to be the leader that Somerville is now.

Also, it would be nice to finally take a vacation after three years without one. Now, let's look at your contract. . . .[*By asking this question, our salesperson has helped the customer move beyond her fears and onto her desires. The customer now sees a link between the salesperson and the future success of the company, as well as future success for the customer herself.*]

You may be wondering why our salesperson continued to ask vision questions after it was clear that a sale was in the works. It is not enough to go through your business life making single, shortsighted sales. A better strategy is to form relationships, to position yourself as a partner, and to see the sale through to the end and beyond.

The bonding that occurred between Samantha and Diane over Greenville's future and Diane's place in it will translate into loyalty and trust down the road. Besides that, these questions allowed Samantha to get to the root of her customer's desires. It is only through a real understanding of a customer and her situation that everyone's needs are met. This not only allows for a tailored response at the outset but also ensures that the relationship will endure beyond the signing of the contract.

9

Try It Yourself:

A Sales Scenario to Sharpen Your Questioning Skills

THIS BOOK HAS introduced you to numerous tools you can use to increase the quality of your business interactions and build real relationships with your customers. Now you will practice using those tools together. As you go through the exercises in this chapter, notice that there are no hard-and-fast rules regulating the order of questions. For example, you might find that opening with an educational question will work in some instances but not others. The key to using these questions lies in listening to the customers and then responding to their concerns, ideas, and frustrations.

Instead of using an example of one of the salespeople introduced in previous chapters, this chapter focuses on you. *You* will be the salesperson navigating the business situation, creating questions appropriate for the customer. I have chosen a scenario that is simple and generic, so you can focus on formulating good questions without having to acquire a lot of product knowledge. Similar situations could be encountered in virtually any business-to-business situation.

The purpose of this book has been to help you in your business-to-business selling. This scenario is a way for you to apply all of the questioning strategies you've learned in a complex environment—one that includes multiple calls, several business personalities, and complex analysis. Your goals should be to:

1. Obtain a genuine understanding of the company's decisionmaking process.
2. Learn the criteria used by key players in the company.
3. Understand the motivating forces behind the customer's decisions.

The Scenario

Your company, General Financial, specializes in commercial leasing. Your division focuses on leasing cars and trucks. Companies might, for example, lease a fleet of vans for their service crews, or lease cars for a field sales organization.

General started only ten years ago and already competes with numerous third-party commercial leasing firms, as well as with leading financial institutions. One of your key challenges is that the leasing industry is commodity driven. To customers, all leases seem pretty much the same. All third-party leasing companies can lease virtually any make or model. So typically, the buying decision comes down to whoever can provide the best terms at the best price.

Your company tries to distinguish itself from the competition by offering value-added solutions and superior service. Your company has a good reputation, and you've developed many personal relationships in the industry, not only with prospects and customers but also with other players, such as auto dealers and body shops. As the sales agent in charge of commercial leasing, you have access to thousands of cars and trucks at a moment's notice—but so do your competitors.

Recently, you've done business with a real estate company that needs cars for approximately fifty real estate agents. You've also done a special deal with a cosmetics company that needed a fleet of purple luxury sedans. You not only recommended the type of sedan, but arranged for custom paint jobs.

Today you receive a memo from your boss concerning a company that needs trucks for hundreds of technicians throughout the United States. The company, Metro Scales, sells and services commercial scales. The leasing company it used in the past recently went out of business and they've invited you to bid on a new contract.

Here's the information your boss provides to you:

Metro Scales is looking for a new leasing agent. It runs a fleet of three thousand trucks. The vice president of the company, Lou Tyler, drives a hard bargain. He has basically run the company for the last twenty-two years because the president would rather spend his days in Saint Tropez.

The sales technicians are the heart of the company. They are the ones who install the scales and fix them when they break down. The technicians cannot get anywhere without their trucks. They rely on them to transport not only scales but also their test weights (which are used to calibrate the scales) and their tools.

You need to find a contact in the company to get your foot in the door. Otherwise, General Financial will be lost among the big-name banks. You have to be careful not to step on anyone's toes, because there has been talk of a merger between Metro Scales and another major scale company, which has made Metro's employees nervous.

Exercise 1

Prepare a list of questions for Vanessa O'Reilly, who is in charge of transportation for Metro Scales. She is the one who must deal with the technicians' complaints about breakdowns or other problems with reliability. If the trucks do not run smoothly, Vanessa is not happy.

You have a phone meeting scheduled with Vanessa, during which you hope to engage her and uncover some valuable information about her company's needs. Vanessa has agreed to speak with you, but she's told your boss that her company will probably go with a major bank. Vanessa will probably be your only path into Metro Scales. But if you can get Vanessa on your side, you will have gone a long way toward completing this sale.

In the spaces below, compile some possible questions to ask Vanessa in the upcoming meeting. (In the parentheses, you are reminded to include several different types of questions and address various business influences.)

1. (An expansion question that addresses internal customers)

   _____

   _____

2. (A question that uncovers performance pressures, such as pressure to reduce overhead or increase profits, or bottlenecks causing constraints on the customer's time)

   _____

   _____

3. (A comparison question that addresses satisfaction with the previous vendor)

   _____

   _____

4. (A vision question that addresses goals for the company as
   well as Vanessa's career goals)

   _____

   _____

After talking with Vanessa, you have discovered the following things:

1. **Vanessa was** extremely unhappy with the previous vendor and was
   glad to see them go. The technicians constantly came to her with
   truck problems, complaining about having to take their vehicles in
   to be serviced and then missing out on overtime because they did
   not have access to replacement vehicles. She also complained that
   the previous vendor was slow to get her new vehicles, sometimes
   taking up to six months to provide a truck to a new technician.

2. **Upper management** has put pressure on Vanessa consistently over
   the last two years because of low productivity in her department.
   Vanessa tried again and again to explain that the problem was with
   the trucks and not her people. After two years, she was vindicated
   when the current vendor filed for bankruptcy.

3. **The company** was losing a good amount of money each year because of truck breakdowns and how long trucks were out of service while waiting for repairs. Vanessa tells you that, on average,
   three trucks break down each day (out of three thousand trucks
   nationwide). This translates to fifteen trucks per week and fifteen
   technicians complaining to Vanessa. She estimates that she has to
   spend twelve hours per week simply keeping the trucks up and
   running, and one person in Vanessa's office dedicates all her time
   to rescheduling appointments because of truck breakdowns.

4. **Vanessa feels** that Lou Tyler (the company's vice president) has
   always respected her, but the chief of operations, Tim Daly, has
   often refused to acknowledge how important transportation is to
   Metro Scales's survival. Rather than focusing on the need for reliable transportation, Daly puts all of his attention into increasing
   productivity and reaching sales and service quotas.

5. **The merger talk** around Metro Scales has reached a fever pitch and
   Vanessa fears her job might be downsized if the merger takes place.

Exercise 2

Using the information you have learned from Vanessa, construct impact questions that will highlight the problems of the current vendor.

1. Impact question #1 (Hint: impact on customers)

_____

_____

2. Impact question #2 (Hint: impact on the company)

_____

_____

3. Impact question #3 (Hint: impact on Vanessa and her ability to get her work done)

_____

_____

Owing to your insightful questions and engagement of Vanessa O'Reilly, you have been able to secure a "sit-down" with her and Tim Daly. The meeting will take place a week from today, so you need to gather information about the current state of affairs in the scale industry. You also need to formulate questions to ask Tim Daly so that you will be able to move the sale forward.

From your research you have found that the scale industry has been growing steadily over the last several years, and Metro Scales has been doing relatively well.

Sales of new scales generally depend on the state of the economy. If businesses are expanding, they buy more scales; if businesses are suffering, they don't need new scales. Metro Scales also generates a good deal of revenue from its contracts—companies with a large number of scales often purchase a service contract that entitles them to around-the-clock service and a set rate for repairs.

As Vanessa O'Reilly told you, the scale business cannot function without trucks. Trucks get the technicians, their tools, and the scales to the customers. Customers, especially those with service contracts, want their scales fixed now! Excuses about trucks being repaired or not enough trucks for each technician ring hollow to customers who are losing money every minute their scales are out of commission.

After your initial meeting with Vanessa and your stellar use of the impact questions, Vanessa called you with more precise information. She told you that a full 5 percent of customer calls currently require rescheduling because of truck problems. Each technician has approximately 120 customers, and on average each customer is worth $20,000 per year to Metro Scales. (*Hint: This is great information to help you quantify the problem.*)

Now that you have all of this information at your disposal, you need to formulate some possible questions for Tim Daly, chief of operations. Daly's main responsibilities include supervision of the ten regional managers and keeping an eye on the bottom line. Vanessa has told you that Daly responds to numbers, especially those with dollar signs in front of them.

Exercise 3

Prepare your questions for Tim Daly, chief of operations. Remember to use the information you learned from Vanessa, as well as from your own research:

1. An expansion question dealing with the bottom line (*Hint: Consider what Vanessa told you about Tim's priorities, such as employee productivity, sales quotas, and the amount of time technicians spend with each of their customers.*)

   _____

   _____

2. A comparison question addressing expectations of a vendor (*Hint: Invite them to compare their current experience with an ideal one.*)

   _____

   _____

3. A qualifying or comparison question concerning the decisionmaking process (*Hint: Try to uncover the different sets of buying criteria among the decisionmakers.*)

   _____

   _____

4. An expansion or comparison question related to external customers (*Hint: This is a great opportunity to create a sense of urgency by shining the light on the qualities customers want from Metro Scales but are not currently getting. The information you gather will*

lead you to the next question when you quantify the problem and its impact on the company.)

_____

_____

5. A question that quantifies the problem (*Hint: Focus on how the problem is negatively affecting Metro Scales.*)

_____

_____

6. A vision question (*Hint: Invite the buyer to dream about a better situation.*)

_____

_____

As you prepare for your meeting with Tim Daly, you call him to ask if there are any particular areas of concern that he would like you to address during your presentation. He tells you, "I need to see an increase in profit by 10 percent over the next quarter and I do not want to have to worry about transportation—this should not have to be my major concern."

Exercise 4

Use Tim Daly's statement to construct lock-on questions. You should be able to write at least four lock-on questions from this one statement. I have given you an example to help jog your memory.

Example: Tim, you mentioned that you want to see an increase in profit by 10 percent. How do others in the company share your vision regarding short- and long-term goals?

1. _____

_____

2. _____

_____

3. _____

_____

4. _____

_____

After meeting with Vanessa and Tim, you are buoyed by the impact you appear to have made on this tough-to-please businessman. Here is what you have found out:

1. **The company** has been losing a lot of money without realizing it. Tim estimated that the company has 360,000 customers across the nation. You related Vanessa's information that 5 percent of calls had to be rescheduled and you calculated that this translates to 18,000 unhappy customers per year. Tim commented that probably 10 percent of those 18,000 customers (which is 1,800 customers) leave every year and go to Metro Scales's competition because of scheduling delays; together you computed a total loss of $36 million per year (when an average customer is worth $20,000 per year). This was eye-opening for Tim.

2. **Although Tim** did not really appreciate the magnitude of the problems Vanessa and the technicians were encountering with the current vendor, he did recognize that the company's productivity was suffering because of these problems. When he learned that fifteen technicians each week were sitting around waiting for their trucks to be repaired, he was furious. He estimated this issue alone cut into productivity and cost Metro Scales $2 million a year. You notice that Vanessa has a small smile on her face—you've gotten Tim to acknowledge something she's been trying to tell him for a long time.

3. **In the meeting,** Vanessa commented that the current vendor's trucks were getting only sixteen miles per gallon. Metro Scales is currently spending $9 million each year on gas for its technicians.

4. **Tim was slow** to open up to you, but eventually he revealed that Metro Scales was falling short of its sales and service quotas by nearly 15 percent. He also told you that Lou Tyler, the company's vice president, had recently questioned him about this problem.

Now you are getting the golden opportunity: the chance to meet with Lou Tyler and show him what General Financial can do for Metro Scales. During your meeting with Lou, you will need to do a couple of things:

Summarize all of the numbers and calculations you have learned from talking with Vanessa and Tim. Remember to lay out all of the ways Metro

Scales has been losing money by dealing with the current vendor. Highlight the ways that General Financial could reduce or eliminate these losses and therefore increase Metro Scales's profits.

Take Lou through another series of impact questions, this time dealing with the issue of spending on gas for the trucks. Inform Lou that General Financial has access to new trucks with a gas mileage of twenty-four miles per gallon, which alone could save him on average $3 million each year.

Disclose the fact that your company's leasing services will cost Metro Scales 25 percent more each year than it was paying its current vendor, but be sure to remind Lou of the savings he will derive from your company and that the net gain will be millions of dollars.

Exercise 5

This is the ultimate test of your skills. You will be talking to the vice president of the company—the person empowered to sign off on the final decision. Ensure that your questions not only illustrate how much money the company is losing right now because of its current leasing contract but also how much money the company stands to gain by doing business with General Financial.

1. Provide a series of impact questions dealing with gas mileage and how it is affecting Metro Scales's bottom line.
2. Develop a question about Metro Scales's competitors, highlighting the 1,800 customers lost each year due to cancellations.
3. Draw up a series of vision questions concerning Lou's personal and business goals.
4. Plan a question about the talk of a merger—what that could mean to Lou, and how General Financial could help Metro Scales's financial situation going into the merger.
5. Propose a qualifying question (see Chapter 10) concerning Lou's readiness to complete this deal.

By now you have probably come to the realization that this type of selling does not eliminate all complications. There are still problems that could arise and personal matters that might interfere with the sale. But you're no longer selling on price in a race to the bottom. You have all of these tools at your disposal, and you should be able to anticipate objections, alleviate fears, and motivate your customers to make a decision. Whether you use an educational question, an impact question, or a qualifying question, you'll find that, after practicing these techniques, you will certainly have an edge over your competition.

10

Qualifying Questions:

Get Prospects to Tell You Why *You* Should Do Business with *Them*

AS A SALESPERSON, you need to be especially vigorous about how you spend your workday. If you devote several hours to writing up a proposal for a prospective customer only to be given the brush-off, no one is going to compensate you for this lost time. Your valuable hours should not be wasted on those who have no interest in pursuing a substantive business relationship. To prevent these time-loss situations from occurring (or at least from occurring too much), you need to *qualify* each of your sales opportunities.

Qualifying means determining whether the sales opportunity is legitimate or simply a waste of time. As a salesperson, you are probably familiar with the following responses to your inquiries:

"Send me more information."
"Call me back."
"Give me a quote."
"Let me run your ideas by my boss."
"How about I let you bid on a project in the future?"
"Why don't you talk it over with the buyer?"
"Can you give us a demo?"

All of these responses require you as a salesperson to exert effort. The last one could even require a trip out of town and expending money and time. Yet none of these requests signals a firm commitment from the prospective customer. Most require little or no effort on the part of the prospective customer. They may indicate legitimate interest, or they may be no more than a polite way for someone to get you off of the phone or out of her office.

The reality is that people are not always forthright with their answers—especially when they're talking to a salesperson. Here are some of the reasons why:

- They are afraid to say no.
- They don't trust you.
- They don't like you.
- They were raised to be polite and don't want to hurt your feelings.
- They want to avoid an argument or confrontation with you.
- They're feeling manipulated or pressured.
- They don't want to look stupid.
- They lack the confidence to make a decision.
- They want to get information from you mainly in order to renegotiate with their current vendor.
- They think there might be problems down the road with their current vendor and want to keep their options open.
- They want to keep you at a distance so that they can maintain power and control.
- They have had a bad experience with a vendor in the past and are afraid to repeat it.

Before you start chasing opportunities, listen to how prospective customers respond to your questions. The process of qualifying allows you to answer these questions:

- Is the person politely trying to get you off of the phone and out of his hair?
- Is this someone who really wants to purchase your services, or is she just picking your brain for free ideas?
- Is he afraid of any type of commitment?
- Is your timing off? Does the person you are talking with have more pressing needs than the one you are addressing?
- Is the prospect open to change and willing to talk about it?
- Are you talking with the right person?
- Are your values aligned with their values (for example, are they price-driven when you're focused on solving problems and providing a return on investment)?

Often salespeople go forward without knowing the answers to any of these questions. Sometimes it comes from anxiety about their pipeline, combined with a big dose of wishful thinking. Or salespeople think it would be rude to ask qualifying questions. Or that it's best not to be intrusive. Or they are in a hurry. And sometimes salespeople just don't know what to ask.

It's in everyone's interest—the buyer as well as the seller—to make sure you're not wasting time on an "opportunity" that isn't there. Real buyers don't mind your efforts to qualify them—their time is valuable, too. And many appreciate that you are being forthright in your approach. So you need to prepare a list of questions that you can ask in order to learn more about your customers' needs.

But what happens when you ask those questions and you get nowhere? You need a process that will help you determine which customers to continue to engage and which ones are likely to be a waste of your time.

Interpreting Prospective Customers' Answers

Here are some of the things you should be looking for in a prospect's answers before you expend time and energy working on a proposal, making a presentation, emailing a prospectus, or getting into the car for a long drive to a prospect's office.

Can your prospect articulate her needs? Any response to a question about needs should tell you whether the prospect has a good working knowledge of the problem and if she has researched possible solutions. If not, this may indicate a lack of interest in your service. Or, it may mean that you're speaking to the wrong person. If this is the case, your task as the salesperson is to locate the individual who has to deal with the problem and has a vested interest in it being solved. After speaking with the person closest to the problem, you should be able to determine whether a legitimate business opportunity exists.

Is this need important? A prospect's response should inform you whether or not there is a sense of urgency. Does this problem have priority over other needs? Find out why or why not. If the need is not important, the prospect may not feel compelled to pursue your service.

How do you determine if a need is important? Ask your prospect a series of questions:

1. How important is this issue to you?
2. What areas of your business does this affect?
3. Can you give me a specific example so that I can really understand the problem you are experiencing?
4. In addition to you, who else is affected by this problem?
5. What steps have been taken to resolve it?
6. What discussions have taken place within your organization around this problem?
7. What have you tried in the past that didn't work?
8. What's the impact of this problem on your business (time, resources, productivity, employee turnover, customer growth and retention, profits, market share, reputation, etc.)?

If your prospect can answer most of these questions with specific details and examples, then you can be sure this is a legitimate opportunity. If the need isn't perceived to be important, you may be able to create urgency with the right follow-up questions. But you'll need to guard your time and energy with this prospect.

How does the prospect envision the outcome of resolving this matter? In other words, what would it mean for the prospect to solve this problem? How would correcting a situation enable your prospect to do something that is desired? What you really want to understand is the *motivation* that will drive your prospect to action. By gaining a better understanding of your prospect's reasons for pursuing your potential solution, you will be better able to create a plan of action. Be careful that your questions don't come across as self-serving. If the prospective customer feels you are being manipulative, he will justifiably feel uncomfortable divulging sensitive information.

If your prospective customer is unwilling to share his motivation with you by answering your questions, one of two things is almost certainly happening: (1) you don't have a legitimate opportunity to pursue or (2) you've failed to build trust and demonstrate empathy, the two key elements that get people to open up.

Responding to the Answers: The Three-Step Qualifying Process

Use the following three-step process to determine whether or not you have a real sales opportunity. This process will save you time and money and help you avoid frustration.

Agree. Most salespeople are quite agreeable and accommodating. After all, you're in the people-pleasing business. For example, if someone says, "Call me back," you're not going to say no. You'll be respectful and agree to a better time to reconnect. If someone says, "I want to think about what you're proposing," you're not going to bark back, "No, you need to decide right now." You'll politely inquire when you should get back to them.

I'm all for being pleasant, accommodating, and supportive. But you walk a fine line. If you're too nice, you'll fail to get decisions. You won't find out how buyers really feel. You won't know whether a sale is going forward or you're spinning your wheels. If all you do is agree, you're traveling down a slippery slope at full throttle. The prospect says, "Get back to me," but you can never get hold of them again. They say "call me," but don't pick up. And when you do get hold of them, they whine about how busy they are and blow you off yet again.

So by all means agree with what the prospect says. But don't stop there. To stay in control, go to the next step: clarify.

Clarify. After agreeing to some part of the prospective customer's initial statement, get as much detail as possible about the response. Ask one or two questions to gather information about the current situation, the decisionmaking process within the company, and any concerns the person has about the current vendor.

Legitimize. Determine whether the prospect is sincere or just trying to get rid of you politely. Ask a question that will project your prospective customer into the future and will allow you to make evident any potential obstacles to an agreement. For example, sometimes prospects ask me to come to their facility or meet in person. I am usually happy to oblige, unless I have to drive more than five hours or hop on a plane and go halfway across the country. In those cases, it becomes a real time-management issue for me. Before I commit to such a trip, I spend significant time on the phone asking the prospect clarifying questions to better understand his needs. I ask, "Let's just assume that I come out to your facility for a day. You're able to pull a group of people together, we do a demo, and everyone really finds value in what we have to offer. What do you see happening next?"

I can get all types of responses, but basically they come down to one of two: (1) "We would do business with you," or (2) "We would have to run it by our boss, or committee, or corporate . . . or . . . we would have to see if we could get the money . . . or . . . we would have to compare you with our current vendor . . . or . . . we're not really sure." If I get the first response (and have determined that the person I'm speaking to actually has that authority), I am on the next plane. If I get the second response, I hesitate to commit my time and resources because there are obstacles in the way over which I have no control. So first I need to find a way to remove those obstacles. If I can clear away issues using the phone and email, it will be easier to get a commitment once I have met the prospect face-to-face. This approach helps ensure that my time—and the prospect's, for that matter—is well spent.

Putting the Process to Work

Now let's look at a few common responses from prospects and see how you can use this qualifying process to determine whether it's worth your time to move forward:

"Email Me the Information."

Do you often get this response when you call a prospective customer? After all the effort you expend getting through voice mail and on the phone with an actual person, it can be deflating. Or, even worse, you convince yourself that the prospect is really interested and jump through hoops, only to be disappointed by the subsequent lack of commitment.

Here is how to use the three-step qualifying process when you encounter this response:

Agree. Find something within the prospect's reply with which you can agree. In this case, you could say something like, "I would be glad to forward you some information."

Clarify. Next, get some clarification about needs. A good example would be, "So that I get you the right information, what specifically are you looking for?" You could also ask, "What specific information would be of particular interest to you?" Or, "I want to be attentive to what your needs are; what kind of information is going to be most beneficial to you?"

Now, the important thing to do is analyze the response. You are looking for the *reason* someone wants information about your product.

Chances are good that this is a genuine opportunity if the prospective client answers a clarification question using words like these: "We're looking to . . . *achieve* . . . *fix* . . . *solve* . . . *eliminate* . . . *avoid* . . . *secure* . . . *improve*. . . . " These kinds of words suggest that this company has already identified its problems and accepted that change is necessary. While the prospective customer explains the problem, listen to gain a better understanding of the goals and the solutions that are being sought, and whether you can provide those solutions.

If the prospective customer answers your clarification questions with something like, "Send me whatever you have," or "I really don't know, I just want to see what you offer," this is probably not a legitimate opportunity. That's a canned response and the prospect is trying to get rid of you, or you've failed to identify what's important to him, or this person just doesn't have a need. Clarifying questions allow you to understand whom best to focus your energy and time with.

Assuming you've gotten clarity, the next step is to legitimize the opportunity.

Legitimize. The final step in the qualifying process compels you, as a salesperson, to project your prospective customer into the future so that she can walk you through the decisionmaking process in her company.

Assuming they opened up about some issues they have and assuming that you have potential solutions, you might say, "I'm going to put together some information that will address x, y, and z, and get that to you today. Let me ask you, assuming what I put together addresses what you're looking for, what's our next step?"

You will be able to discern from the answer whether or not there is any real interest from this company. For example, a well-qualified buyer may respond something like this: "Well, if you proposed something that looked like it might work, I'd ask you to come in and meet with me and my team to get deeper into the issues." (Indeed, if you got a response like this or something similar, you'd probably want to take it one step further and insist on scheduling an appointment, in order to avoid phone tag later on.)

On the other hand, if all you got were blow-off responses such as "I don't know" during the clarifying phase, there's no need to try to move forward with this person (though you may want to move forward with someone *else* in the organization). Either he or she has no power, doesn't care, or is working a hidden agenda (for example, using you to get a better price from the current vendor). You've called the person's bluff, but without being confrontational.

Some phrases with which you can begin legitimizing questions include:

"Assuming we can . . ."

"What if . . ."

"Let's just pretend . . ."

"Just suppose . . ."

"Imagine for a moment . . ."

You can then end your legitimizing questions with the phrase, "What do you feel will happen next?" Using these key phrases at the beginning and end of your questions, you will be able to confirm how your prospective customer envisions what it will take to do business with her, as well as any hurdles to clear or objections to overcome.

You do have the option to be more direct and go for a close if the clarifying phase is going well. For example, if the buyer clearly seems engaged and is asking detailed questions, you might say something like this: "I suggest the next step should be a meeting with you. How is next Tuesday at 10:00 a.m. or Thursday at 2:00 p.m.?"

Here's another possible scenario:

Salesperson: "I'll get this proposal to you on Monday. How does that work with your schedule? Also, assuming we can address your needs regarding _____ and stay within your budget of _____ , tell me what you see as a next step."

Or you can go for a firm yes or no response: "Assuming we can address your needs regarding _____ , and stay within your budget of _____ , are you prepared to move forward?"

You can use countless variations of this language:

"If this is a good solution for you and it's within your budget . . . "

". . . does that mean I will have earned your business?"

". . . how soon can we get started?"

". . . will we able to formalize the agreement tomorrow?"

". . . can I stop by this Friday to pick up the check?"

". . . when would we see the purchase order?"

Sounds awfully direct, doesn't it? But keep in mind that if your prospect is asking you to do something that requires your time and effort and your company's resources, why can't you ask for the buyer to share *their* level of commitment? It's a fair question.

It's also a revealing one. They are either going to give you a yes—and if so, congratulations—or going to hem and haw, or they're going or let you know the truth as to where they are in the buying process. Their response will allow you to gauge how easy or hard the sale is going to be.

Let's continue with this example:

Prospective client: I have no idea. As a matter of fact, I tried suggesting something like this before and the board shot it down.

Ugh! If you hear something like that, it's best to pull back immediately from doing a proposal. At best, you have a lot more work to do before you get to the proposal stage.

A response like that isn't what you want to hear, but it's enormously valuable. It helps you get at hidden objections. It doesn't mean that this opportunity is a dead end, but the situation is obviously complex. In all likelihood you're not talking to the right person, and he is probably far removed from the powers that be. You can either walk away from this prospect to focus on more promising opportunities, or use further clarification questions to gain insight into the decisionmaking process, the issues, proposed solutions, and get yourself connected to somebody who can make something happen.

Salespeople sometimes worry about going over the prospect's head, but at this point you don't have anything to lose. In fact, if prospects *admit* that they lack power, they may actually *want* you to talk to someone who does. So you might ask, for example: "Who shot it down and why?" And, "If this idea had any chance of success, who on the board would have to get behind it?"

Here's another possible scenario:

Salesperson: Assuming we can address your needs regarding _____ and stay within your budget of _____ , tell me what you see as a next step.

Prospective Client: Well, I would bring you in to meet my boss and our team leader.

Hearing this response should immediately signal that there is interest here. By asking the legitimizing question, you learn the next step in the process, as well as who else will be involved in making the decision.

After you have used the three-step qualifying process to determine that your prospect is legitimate, you can go on to ask more questions. Especially if your prospective customer appears to want to continue the dialogue, you can use this opportunity to gain a huge amount of information and secure a commitment for the next step. This strategy saves you time, helps you focus on genuine business opportunities, and gives you more control over the sales process.

A Chain of Questions

The qualifying process involves three steps, but it almost always involves way more than three questions. Good questions lead to more questions. Each question in the chain gives you more valuable insights. Even more important, it helps the prospect think more deeply about the sales process and what has to happen to get what he wants.

Here's an example of a chain of qualifying questions:

"Based on what I have presented to you, what do you like the most about what we've discussed?"

Notice that I want to know where he stands. Is this person engaged enough to identify one or two key areas that get him motivated? Or are you going to get a blow-off such as, "I like everything," or "It all sounds good"?

Let's say the prospect responds like this: "Well, what I really like about what we discussed is how it's going to make my job easier and free up a lot of my time that could be better spent in working with my team."

Your next clarifying question might be:

"You mentioned that Mike will be involved in deciding whether to go forward. From Mike's perspective, tell me what you feel will be of most value to him."

The prospect might say: "Mike is all about the bottom line and generating more sales. I think that's what will be of most interest to him."

At this point, take a moment to respond and validate what you've heard: "Great. You're right: It definitely will free up everyone's time so they can do more productive activities and generate more sales."

Next, start to "rehearse" the sales process with your buyer:

"So if Mike raises some concerns—for example, if he says he doesn't see how this would increase sales, what would you say to him?"

The prospect might say: "Well, this is something near and dear to me. I spend at least fifteen to eighteen hours a week processing orders that would be off my plate. I'd point out to Mike that this is time I could devote to getting out on sales calls with my team and closing more sales. Don't worry: I know how to sell him on it."

If you get that kind of answer—where the prospect is passionate, takes ownership, and has the confidence to sell the concepts internally—by all means let him or her go for it. But what if you get a response like this: "Well if Mike doesn't see the value, I guess we'll just have to wait and see. He's the boss, and we do what he says"?

You'll hear plenty of these types of frustrating responses. But consider: Your prospect has just given you incredible insight into the dynamics of the organization. You're learning about the relationship between Mike and the prospect. You're learning what kind of resistance may be in store, who really makes the decisions, the prospect's level of confidence, and his ability to sell your ideas. So now you know how to work this sale. You might say:

"Thanks for your candor. So here's what I recommend: The three of us sit down together and go over the pros and cons with this proposed solution. I say this because questions are going to come up. It's important that we get Mike's perspective, how he sees things, and be able to respond to issues he might raise. And I'll be there to support you and address them. What does next week look like for the three of us to get together?"

So why not just ask to meet with Mike in the first place? Because you haven't given the prospect a reason to say yes. By taking him or her through a chain of clarifying questions, you help the prospect arrive at this conclusion on their own. He or she is thinking: "Yeah, I don't want to look stupid in front of Mike. He asks tough questions, and that makes me anxious. If all three of us meet, the pressure is off of me; I trust that you can go in with me and articulate the value. And if there's any push-back or if the boss says no, it'll be on you, not me."

As you can see, the chain of clarifying questions never explicitly asked the buyer to talk about these emotional drivers, but it revealed them all the same. And that allows you to create a powerful sales strategy.

In fact, a big part of the legitimizing process involves motivating prospects to open doors and introduce you to other key decisionmakers in their organization. That demonstrates trust, and that they value the relationship they are starting to build with you. And it instills confidence.

The bottom line is this: When someone gives weak responses and doesn't want to get their boss or others who have a stake in the decision involved, a red flag should go up. It means they don't have a stake in selling your solution internally and will fold at the first sign of push-back. Most likely, they'll come back to you with vague objections, or even worse, stall you with excuses like, "I haven't had time to present it to her," or "I haven't heard anything," or "She's really busy."

Now let's examine some typical situations where you can use the three-step qualifying process.

"I Need to Talk It Over With . . ."

Do you ever feel as if no one wants to make a decision, or that you are always talking to the wrong person in a company? Even though selling to buying groups, boards, or committees is a common scenario today, you must remember that companies do not make decisions—people do. Yet, because of competing interests within an organization, it is often difficult to determine who really has the final say on a purchase and who has the greatest influence during the decisionmaking process.

When you are offered a response such as, "I need to talk it over with Mike," you can use the three-step process that we outlined in the previous example, asking questions that will help clear up some of the confusion.

Agree. Respond to this statement with something like, "Great, I'm happy to hear that you will discuss this with him." You need to remember, however, not to end the call there. As in the previous example, continue the chain: If you fail to secure a time for that follow-up call or meeting, it is likely that this prospective client may not be motivated to pass your information along to the decisionmaker.

Clarify. Get some more information from your prospective customer. Make sure that you obtain a time frame within which the action will occur, as well as some specifics about the impending interaction.

If your prospective customer cannot or will not answer your clarifying question, this is probably not a legitimate business opportunity.

"Call Me Back in Three Months"

Unfortunately, there aren't prospective customers sitting at their desks this very minute waiting for you to call. It should not surprise you, then, that many people are busy when you call them out of the blue. What is important to remember is that you cannot assume anything from this response.

"Call me back" is one of the most difficult answers to decipher. Sometimes a prospect might really be busy, maybe even in the middle of a crisis, and she has absolutely no time to talk. If you get this response, ask for a specific time to call back. If a prospect is willing to give you that consideration, then there might be a business opportunity. If not, you might want to move on to the next prospect.

When you hear "Call me back in three months," do you know whether or not the prospective customer is interested in your service? No. In most cases, the response is a knee-jerk reaction by a buyer who wants to avoid a decision or is assuming what you are selling is of little or no value. It's easier than giving you an absolute no, or thinking about whether this is something they might need. "Call me back" creates the illusion that they've kept their options open. But with few exceptions, nothing will happen over the next three months that will make this decision any easier. In fact, you've probably experienced numerous times that when you do follow up at the time they suggested, you get the same canned reply, "I'm busy, call me back." And that's if you are lucky enough to have even got a hold of them. Right?

So you need to find out more information from this person to evaluate whether you should spend your valuable time calling him again or cut your losses. Here is how the three steps help you do this:

Agree. Whether it's a prospect or a current customer, when you hear, "Call me back at a later date," common sense dictates that you first go along with this request. Although it may sound trivial, make sure that you agree to that request and set a specific time for your return phone call. This minimizes the risk of calling back at a time when the prospect has other commitments or is away from the office. Otherwise, you'll get trapped in voice mail phone tag and might spend another two months calling him back.

Clarify and legitimize. "Call me back" is a great example in which you do not always have to follow the three-step approach systematically. Responding to "call me back" allows you to combine your clarify and legitimize questions, giving you flexibility on how to engage your prospects.

Here are some additional qualifying questions to ask:

"So that I can best prepare my follow-up call, what exactly will we be discussing?" [assuming he knows who you are].

"As I plan my next call with you, what will be occurring between now and the next three months?" [or the time frame he gave you].

"So that I am attentive to you when I follow up, what do you have in mind that we should be prepared to talk about?"

You must now quickly evaluate whether or not the answers to your clarifying questions suggest a legitimate business opportunity or a vast black hole in which you would be wasting hours of your time. A prospective customer who can cite specific problems he wants to address, such as low productivity or troubles in human resources, shows that he recognizes the value of your service and should be classified as a legitimate opportunity. His answer would be something like, "When you call me back, I would like to discuss how we can streamline our shipping process because we have been losing business owing to delays in this area."

Another legitimate opportunity would involve a situation in which an important person who should be involved in evaluating your proposal is currently on vacation or on a business trip. A prospective client might say, "John, our shipping supervisor, who needs to assist me in making this decision, is traveling, but he will be back within the next few weeks and I would like his input."

You can continue to clarify and legitimize at this point, with questions like these:

"What do you perceive will be of most interest to John?"

"What key points will you be stressing to him?"

"What concerns do you think John will have?"

After asking any of these questions, follow up with a legitimizing question to evaluate how committed your prospective customer is to going forward. Some options include: "Assuming John likes what he hears, what do you think will happen next?" or "Imagine John is not receptive. How do you think you would respond?" You can have a little fun with this and propose some potential objections to test how solid the contact's support is for your proposal—for example, "Do you think John is going to have time to work on this problem when he gets back?"

These questions should provide you with enough information to conclude that the call has potential.

Unfortunately, you will not always get to this stage in an initial sales call. There will be many times when a legitimate sales opportunity does not exist. In most cases, "Call me back" will be a blow-off, but it's worth asking a few more questions to be sure.

Some experts will suggest that if a prospect says he or she is too busy to talk, you shouldn't even try to engage them. In my view, however, a prospect who's willing to pick up the phone instead of letting the call go to voice mail isn't *that* busy, and many will give you the opportunity to ask a couple of brief questions. Otherwise, good luck trying to reconnect with them at a later date.

The important thing to remember is that by qualifying each call you will tend to spend more time on those prospective clients most likely to do business with you.

"You Really Should Be Talking to Jeanine"

This reply provides a convenient out for many people. The prospective customer relinquishes responsibility and passes it on to Jeanine. Although there may be some instances when this response represents the truth, many times it is simply another way for the prospect to bow out.

You need to tailor your questions to your audience. For example, imagine you are trying to sell software to the president of a large corporation. You have to engage her on how your product will increase profits, reduce overhead, and improve communications. If you start getting into technical language and differences between operating systems, she might simply delegate the decision to a lower-level purchasing agent. A low-level manager will not be as interested in your long-term promises; rather, this person will most likely be more interested in one factor—price. You will have lost a golden opportunity to deal directly with the senior decisionmaker and be left haggling over pennies.

By completing the following exercise, you will have the chance to practice using the three-step qualifying process to determine whether or not you are talking with a genuine prospect.

Exercise 1

The customer says, "You really should be talking to someone else." Write down (or at least formulate in your head) the three steps you should follow to determine if you have a legitimate business opportunity.

Agree. Write down a sentence that agrees with something the person has said.

Clarify. Find out why the person thinks you should be talking to someone else, and what topic the customer feels this other person will be most interested in discussing. Write down your question.

Legitimize. Write down a question that can help you determine whether there's a legitimate opportunity here.

So how did you do? At this point, you should have been able to formulate one response and two questions to elicit information from your prospective client. Here are some examples of good answers to the exercise. Check your questions against these examples to ensure that you have internalized the three-step qualifying process.

Answers to Exercise 1

Agree. Your answer should be positive and concise. "Great! I would be happy to talk to Jeanine!"

Clarify. Your answer should probe the possible interest of the company in your service, the prospect's relationship with Jeanine, or Jeanine's possible interests related to your service: (1) "So that I can prepare for my call with Jeanine, what do you think will be of most interest to her?" Or (2), "I want to be ready for any questions Jeanine might have. What do you see as a benefit to changing your current service?" Or (3), "Based on your past experiences working with Jeanine, how receptive do you think she'll be to considering us?" Or (4), "So that I'll be prepared when I speak to Jeanine, what challenges have you experienced with your current service?"

Legitimize. Your answer should include the two parts of the legitimizing question, as well as prompt consideration on the part of the prospective customer. (1) "Let's assume I get through to Sarah and she likes what she hears. What do you see happening next?" Or (2), "Just pretend for a second that Sarah has read my proposal. Can you think of any concerns she might have?"

Exercise 2

Now you are on your own. Supply your solutions to the following response (one you have probably encountered more than once): "Send me some references."

Agree: _____

_____

Clarify: _____

_____

Legitimize: _____

_____

Answers to Exercise 2

Agree: "I would love to give you a list of our references right now!" (This way you keep the conversation going and do not have to waste time and money sending the information. Also, if you agree to forward the information without any further questioning, you will run the risk of not getting a response from that prospect.)

Clarify: (1) "So that I can have you talk to the right people, what specifically would you like to discuss with these individuals?" Or (2), "I would like to let my references know you will be calling. When do you plan on contacting them?"

Legitimize: "I am sure that you realize that our references

represent our most satisfied customers and will naturally say good
things about us. Let us assume that you have talked to them and
you like what you hear; what do you feel will happen next?"

Why Qualify?

Many books on sales and sales techniques put a great burden on the
salesperson to close every deal, no matter what. This is a mistake. There
will be numerous times when you'll find that there is simply no sale to
be had! By pursuing a sale that does not exist, you risk alienating a potential future customer by making yourself a nuisance. Also, you will
be spending your valuable time and energy without getting anything in
return. This is why the three-step qualifying process is so important. In a
matter of a few minutes, and with some well-constructed questions, you
will be able to evaluate whether or not a prospect has genuine interest in
doing business with you. You will save time and money, not to mention
enormous amounts of aggravation on your part as well as the prospective customer's. Furthermore, the answers you will elicit by using this
process will provide you with invaluable information about your prospect and her company.

Using these answers will allow you to better prepare any proposal you
might submit to this prospect in the future. It will permit you to anticipate the most likely objections your prospect might have, while giving
you an opportunity to address them. Figure 10-1 will help you adapt this
process for many different situations.

FIGURE 10-1

Customer Response	Agree	Clarify	Legitimize	Things to Remember
I need to think it over.	I'm glad to hear you're giving it some thought. After all, it's important that you make the right decision.	Based on what we've discussed, tell me what specifically stands out that is of most interest to you?	Since you need to give it some thought, it tells me you have some concerns. What are they?	When someone says they need to think about it, there is an underlying issue that you need to address. Find out what they like most. Then address their doubts or fears. To avoid them, indecisiveness will take over.
Let me talk it over with....	Great. It's important that you get input from (boss, spouse, colleague).	When will you be speaking with....? When should I get back with you?	Before you talk with ( ) tell me what you like most about what we've discussed? RESPONSE What do you think will be of most interest to ( )? RESPONSE What if he's not receptive, how will you respond?	When a prospect says she needs to talk it over with...your objective is to find out if they are sincerely interested or using someone else as a stall tactic because they are unsure or have little interest to begin with.

Customer Response	Agree	Clarify	Legitimize	Things to Remember
Email me some information.	I would be happy to get you some information about my solutions.	So that I send you the right information, tell me about your current situation. **OR** Tell me what's going on now when it comes to... **OR** What are some specific issues you're looking to address with....?.	I'll pull together some ideas to address specifically what you just shared with me. Assuming you like what you see, what's our next step?.... Let's get something on the calendar now so we can discuss further.	If you spend time emailing or sending information without first deciding if this prospect is an authentic opportunity, or hoping your info does the selling for you so you don't have to, you're wasting time and resources.
Bob would be the best person to talk to in our organization who would look at what you have to offer.	Great. I would be happy to talk with Bob in purchasing.	So that I can prepare my call with Bob, what's been your experience when it comes to dealing with issues regarding.... **OR** Tell me Bob's likes or dislikes when it comes to.... **OR** Based on your relationship with Bob, what do you think will be of most interest to him?	Assuming Bob likes what I share with him, how would you like to be brought back into the conversation?	This is an example where your contact is brushing you off to someone else in his organization. **OR** You are dealing with an organization where no one wants to make a decision. Gain insight on what the relationship is between these two people

10-1 continued...

Customer Response	Agree	Clarify	Legitimize	Things to Remember
Send me a quote.	Sure. I'd be happy to get that to you right away.	So I can best serve you, tell me about your current situation. Hoping to accomplish? Needs? Budget? Timing? Who else involved?	I'll get to work on this quote. Based on what you shared with me, assuming we come back and meet your requirements including pricing and turnaround, what's our next step? **OR** Is it fair to say you'll give me the business?	When salespeople overlook asking basic qualifying questions to determine if a prospect is serious or just doing a price check to keep his current vendor honest, it becomes a time waster. Close them before you submit the quote and not afterwards.
Call me back....	I would be happy to call you back....	Let's schedule a specific time on the calendar and have a conversation....	So that I can address what's important to you, what is it that we should plan to discuss? **OR** What is it you want to address when I call you back?	Many times when someone says, "Call me back," she really means, "This is not important" or "I have no interest." Make sure there is a purpose to your follow up call and not just checking in.

10-1 continued

11

Alien Encounters:

Questions for the First Meeting That Get Buyers to Open Up

DEVELOPING ANY RELATIONSHIP is a process, something that takes time and effort. Trying to force or manipulate a relationship into a specific time frame can backfire and cause one or both of the parties involved to quit the relationship. This is just as true for business relationships as for personal relationships. In order to cultivate trust and success, you need to invest time in the process by asking the right questions of your clients and prospective clients.

Just as important as asking questions, however, is being patient and listening to the rich information that comes your way in the form of answers. Doing so will instill confidence and trust in the prospective clients, the foundation upon which to build powerful business relationships. In this chapter, you will learn about the vital areas to explore when getting to know your clients.

Preparation

Putting together a list of questions before a sales call is essential. That's because your strategy begins with determining what information you need.

Before meeting with a prospective client, always do your homework. In addition to Google, LinkedIn, Facebook, Twitter, and similar sources, consider online business directories, such as Hoovers, Dun & Bradstreet, Data.com, Charlie, or WHOIS. (Of course, the sources of information are constantly changing and growing, and this should by no means be considered a comprehensive list.) These resources are especially useful for understanding industry trends, a company's rank in its industry, its financial strength, its executives and their backgrounds, its competitors, and its customer base. The more detailed information you can compile, the more personalized your questions can be.

If the prospect contacted you and you're calling back, also prepare questions to find out what prompted his interest and what is on his mind. For example, is it a pressing matter, an idea he is just kicking around, or simply a tactic to keep his current vendor honest?

The First Meeting

Whether in person or on the phone, you want to make a great first impression. So what should you do in the first few minutes of the meeting? Do you jump right into questioning if the prospect knows little about you? How do you provide some background on your company without falling into the trap of doing a sales pitch?

When it comes to building rapport with a prospect, you want to build credibility quickly and set the stage. Otherwise the prospect may ask herself, "Why am I wasting my time with this salesperson?" Because these first moments are so important, it's important to prepare a "value opening statement" ahead of time, and to practice it until you can deliver it flawlessly.

The value opening statement is sometimes called your credibility statement, unique sales proposition, or elevator speech (because you have a short window to catch a prospect's attention—about the time you might spend on an elevator with someone—before she decides whether she wants to continue the dialogue or not).

How do you condense all the sales information in your brain into a brief commercial that will leave your prospect wanting to hear more? Here's one template you can use:

Spend the first eight seconds explaining briefly what your company does or highlighting a specialty that gets the prospect's attention.

Then introduce a recent client success story. Prospects relate to stories. Best of all, stories connect with a prospect's emotions. Just make sure that the story is relevant, specific, short, and results-oriented (that is, in dollars, percentages, or numbers).

Below is a four-step process to get the meeting going so you can easily transition to the questioning stage and get the prospect to open up:

1. Introductions and pleasantries: Start with your value opening statement. If it's on the phone, this introduction should be very

brief—just a sentence or two (think of an online ad on YouTube).
If you're meeting face-to-face, you still must be brief (thirty seconds to two minutes). All you want to do is give a buyer a point
of reference and some context for your call. Then you want to
shift the focus to the buyer.

2. Assessment: Learn about the prospect and their organization—
   their needs and challenges.
3. Evaluation: Determine (jointly with the prospect) whether there's
   a good fit.
4. Next steps: Assuming there's a potential fit, identify next steps.

By the way, there's no need for a hidden agenda here. Prospects already know you're a salesperson! So make this process completely trans-
parent to your prospect, whether it's on a cold call or in a face-to-face
meeting. If you describe the four steps, prospects will know that they're
not in for a long, meandering conversation. And they'll be more likely
to spend time with you when they see that you're focused, purposeful,
efficient, and respectful of their time.

Here is an example of the beginning of a first meeting:

Salesperson: Hi, I'm Paul Cherry [shaking hands as I introduce myself],
with Performance Based Results. [*A few pleasantries are exchanged, and then
I transition into the following.*] Before we get started, would it be helpful if I
spend sixty seconds on exactly who we are and what we do?

Prospect: Sure, go right ahead.

Salesperson: Performance Based Results is a sales development organization. Having worked with more than 1,200 organizations, our goal
is to help companies improve their bottom line by maximizing sales
performance. Are you familiar with Company _____ ? [*It doesn't matter
whether the customer says yes or no; the question allows your introduction to be inter-
active.*] They were frustrated at the lengthy sales cycle of a new product
launch, and turned to us for help. We put together a plan to coach their
sales team on key behaviors linked to specific sales outcomes. After
three months, they were able to reduce their sales cycle by 23 percent
and they documented over $10 million in revenue that they attributed to
our sales training process.

Brevity is important. A great sound bite speaks results in terms of dollars, numbers, or percentages. It should also hit an emotional desire, such as overcoming or avoiding failure and achieving greater success. A full 98 percent of prospects want one or the other.

Once your sound bite is over, resist the urge to sell. In fact, it's important to pull back on the reins. If you appear anxious to sell, your prospect will pick up on that and get anxious, too—which creates defensiveness. Plus, you'll sound like every other salesperson trying to push his solution to the client's problem. The key to establishing a relationship is to shift the focus onto the customer and keep that focus on that customer, not on you.

Salespeople tend to spend way too much time on their value opening statement. It feels like safe ground because they know their products and solutions so well. But you want to provide just enough information to create a context for the conversation, and quickly move on to what buyers truly care about: themselves and their problems. Here's a simple transition you can use:

Salesperson: Whether our process would work for you, I don't know. But if it's okay with you, I would like to ask you some questions to better understand your goals so that I can determine if our solutions are a good fit with your objectives. How does that sound?

The value opening statement allows you to cite your success and then pull back with a statement such as this:

Salesperson: I'm not sure if what we did for Client X is a good fit for you, but to find out more, may I ask you a few questions?

Some salespeople struggle with this approach because they think that saying "I am not sure" will come across as weak or insecure. But it comes across as honesty. The truth is, you don't know whether your solution is a good fit, and it would be presumptuous to pretend otherwise. So this approach achieves two things: It lowers the prospect's resistance ("I'm not going to get a hard sell") and it earns you the right to ask questions ("This salesperson has given me a legitimate reason for her questions").

Asking Permission

Another key step that salespeople often overlook is asking permission to proceed. Either they're too eager to get to the selling part of the conversation, or they're afraid that they'll give a prospect an out. But ask yourself: Will a prospect be more or less willing to engage with you if you ask their permission? What would you do if you were the prospect? Asking permission demonstrates respect. It also signals confidence: Only desperate salespeople try to steamroll a prospect.

Here are some ways to ask:

"Why don't we start out with me giving you a brief overview of who we are and what we do? And then I'd like to get to know you and your needs so I in turn can give you some suggestions on how our services might best address what's important to you. How's that sound?"

"Just as a doctor has to do a proper diagnosis to ensure the right prognosis, it's important that I understand your needs, so that I in turn can make solid recommendations that will address what's important to you. So would it be okay to ask you a few questions?"

"I've worked with other clients in your industry and have some ideas that might work for you. But first let me ask you a few questions."

"With your permission, I'd like to learn more about you and your team's needs. So let me ask you. . . ."

Three Suggestions to Make the First Meeting Go Smoothly

1. **Ease into the conversation with warm-up questions.** Asking about problems at the beginning of the call is risky unless the prospect has volunteered the information beforehand. Although some salespeople like to ask questions about the weather, sports, hobbies, or a familiar object in the prospect's office, these approaches are overused and they waste your time and your client's time. Good warm-up questions are open-ended, broad in scope, and focused on getting the prospect to talk about herself. Here are some examples:

    "How long have you been with this organization?"
    "How did you get into the business?"

"In preparation for my visit with you, I did a little research about your company and discovered that you do _____ exceptionally well. So tell me: How you were able to achieve that?"

"What would you say you like most about your work? Least?"

"If your employees/team/coworkers/customers/etc. were to describe this organization in five words or less, what words would come to mind?" [*Listen to the words given and then respond, "The word _____ is an interesting one; could you elaborate on that for me?"*]

"What would your best customers say are the reasons they enjoy doing business with you?"

Based on the prospect's responses to warm-up questions, you will be able to understand a lot about her interests, personality, beliefs, how she feels about the organization where she works, and the culture of the company in a very short time frame.

2. **Write down the information given to you by your prospective client.** Capture any and all critical information before it escapes your brain. I tend to listen for certain key words and the emotions underlying those words. After you jot those words down, it is much easier to go back and get the prospect to elaborate.

3. **Remove any assumptions you have about this prospect and her problems.** Why do they say new salespeople have beginner's luck? I remember working with a rep who sold high-tech equipment in a complex selling environment. He had been on the job for only six months, yet he closed the biggest deal in the company's history. When he was asked about his secret to success, he admitted that he hardly understood the product. So he simply asked lots of questions!

Was it beginner's luck? I doubt it. It was more likely that he had no assumptions about his client, her problems, or the product. Instead, his curiosity forced him to ask questions that experienced salespeople would have skipped over because they assumed they already knew the answers.

Many salespeople have strong egos—it's what helps them survive the rigors of such a demanding occupation. Yet there is a tendency for people with strong egos to want to talk, and to impress customers with their knowledge and ideas.

Here's a secret: *Your customers love to talk just as much as you do*! If you can ask questions to get your customers talking, you are much more likely to learn how to attend to their needs. Let your customer have the microphone. It's their show. *A good measure of an effective sales call is who did most of the talking.* If it was the prospect, it was a great call. If it was the salesperson, it was a lousy call.

12

More Problems = More Sales

Questions That Enlarge the Need

SOME SALESPEOPLE STOP digging once they've identified one need or pain point. They see an opportunity to sell something and are eager to move on to the next step of the sales process: preparing and presenting solutions. And sometimes salespeople *never* get past that initial problem.

But the first need you identify isn't necessarily the buyer's only need, or even the best one for you to address. Some are disclosed early. Some are revealed only after the buyer has come to trust you, or after the most urgent need has been addressed. Organizations are always growing and changing, so the needs the buyer described to you last week may no longer be relevant, and new problems have taken their place. Discovery must be an ongoing process.

In this chapter, we'll look at some questions that will allow you to dig deeper and uncover additional opportunities. You wouldn't want to use them all at once, or even with every customer. Rather, think of them as a set of tools, and choose the tool that fits the task. And, of course, you'll want to adapt them to fit your personality, the personality of your buyer, the nature of what you sell, and the industry you work in.

Questions to Uncover Problems

How many prospects have you called on who were clueless about the problems they were facing? How many were in a state of complacency about their problems? Or in survival mode? Or hoping that if they could wait it out long enough, the problem would eventually fix itself?

I love finding problems because that means uncovering opportunities. It helps to keep in mind that customers are more motivated to fix their problems than to pursue pleasure. This means that you should dig for problems whenever you can. People are too busy in their everyday lives. They have no time or energy left to step back and assess the actual state they are in because they are caught up in their day-to-day struggles. That is why great salespeople realize the value of becoming trusted business advisers who can help prospects evaluate their current situation and take action before a potential problem erupts.

We all have a preference to stay put. It is human nature. But as sales-people, we need to ask the right questions to open our prospects' minds and get them to think about the risks of staying within their comfort zones.

Be careful about pointing a problem out to your prospects. It's best if they discover it for themselves as they reflect on the answers they give to your questions.

Here are some great problem questions to ask:

- Share with me your three biggest challenges. Of these three, which one is the most pressing?
- What problems are you currently experiencing? Why?
- What is causing these problems? Can you give me an example?
- What barriers are in your way?
- What's working? What's not? Why?
- What's this problem costing you, in terms of time, money, resources, lost opportunities, etc.?
- How long have you been experiencing this problem?
- Who else besides you is experiencing this problem?
- Think back to when you originally implemented this process. What were your expectations? What results are you currently getting? What kind of results would you like to get in the future?
- If you could wind back the clock [or wave a magic wand], what would you change?
- Everyone has to deal with change. What's the one change you [department, organization] are encountering? What challenge is this change presenting?
- What are the biggest gripes you hear from your customers? From your internal customers [bosses, peers, subordinates, or other departments]?

- On a scale from 1 to 10, how satisfied are you with your current product/vendor/situation? What would you like to see the product/vendor/situation do/deliver/accomplish in order to achieve a 10?
- What do you see as the biggest hurdle you face in order to meet your objectives? As you evaluate your current situation, where are the biggest areas or opportunities for improvement?
- What happens if you decide not to fix this problem? What will be the impact on you and your organization?

Questions About Your Customers' (External) Customers

Surprisingly, not every customer you call on is focused on external customers. Unless your clients have direct contact with external customers, too often you will discover how insensitive to or ignorant they are of their external customers' needs. Under these circumstances, it is likely that internal customers will have greater influence. This makes your job twice as difficult because you need to convince your customers that their external customers are important, and you need to uncover the wants and needs of those external customers.

Here are some examples of questions about external customers:

- Who are your organization's most valuable customers?
- Can you give me a profile of your typical client? An ideal client?
- How do your customers measure success as a result of doing business with you?
- Describe for me what an ideal customer looks like.
- What's it going to take to get more of these types of customers?
- What do your customers expect from you as a vendor or supplier? What's the one area where you shine in meeting and/or exceeding their expectations? Where do you see room for improvement?
- How have your customers' expectations changed over the last few years? What changes do you see moving forward?
- What steps will you need to take in order to adapt to those changing expectations?
- Customers have a lot of choices today. What would you say is the #1 reason why they buy from you and not elsewhere?

Be selective to whom you ask these questions. For example, if you asked these questions of a purchasing agent, you would get a blank stare. That's because purchasing has little, if any, interaction with external customers. So, when you ask these questions, make sure they are directed to people who have significant contact with external customers. In addition, people whose jobs are more removed from external customers can have personal or political agendas that conflict with the company's overall goals. That's because they are typically competing with other internal agendas, departments, and budgets.

Questions to Disrupt Existing Vendor Relationships

Nearly every prospect will tell you, "We already have someone who does that for us." After all, if a need exists, the buyer must have some type of solution in place already. (In fact, if they don't, you should ask yourself whether you really have an opportunity.) Sooner or later, you'll have to disrupt these relationships.

Sometimes it's easy—if the buyer is dissatisfied with the current vendor or thinks they might get a better deal with you. Often, though, it's more challenging. You're asking buyers to admit that they might have made a mistake when they chose their current vendor. And you have to be careful not to disparage an existing relationship, while simultaneously planting the seed that there might be something better out there.

Phrase your questions in ways that won't end up undermining your efforts to win your customer's business. For example, don't just ask your customer, "What do you like about your current supplier?" If she's fairly content with the status quo, she just might start talking about all the positive qualities of that relationship. And if things are going just dandy between them, what does she need you for?

Here are better ways to get that information without undermining what you have to offer:

- Would you share with me the ideal qualities you look for in a vendor?
- How's that compare with your current situation?
- When you originally selected this vendor, what were your selection criteria? In what ways have your criteria changed as you evaluate your needs today? What would you like to see happen in the future?

- If you could enhance one thing about your vendor's qualities, what would that be?
- I understand that you have a good relationship with _____. However, different suppliers have different strengths. Could you help me understand where they seem to be meeting your needs and one area they can improve on?
- How would you rate your current vendor relationship on a scale of 1 to 10? (*When your customer states a number, urge her to elaborate.*) All right, when you say 7, what would you want your vendor to do to move it to a 10?

Questions About Competition and Trends

No business can survive without periodically assessing its competition. Similarly, no business can thrive without a keen awareness of the trends affecting its industry. As you serve your customers, you should ask questions about these two very important aspects of business.

These questions will force your customers to focus on the future while critically analyzing their present situation. They will have to ask themselves, "Can I get where I want to go with what I have now?" No matter what the answer, you will have provided them a valuable service by getting them to answer the questions.

Here are some great questions about competition and trends:

- How do you differentiate yourself from your competitors?
- In the next three years, who do you think will emerge as your biggest threat?
- In the next three years, what do you think your greatest opportunity will be?
- Which of your product's or service's strengths will allow you to continue your success?
- How do you picture the direction of your industry in three years? Five years? Ten years?
- What change could cut into your share of the market?
- How does the aging of the baby boomer generation (*for example*) affect your share of the market? (*You could use any applicable trend for this example.*)

- How does your company see itself today? How has it changed over the last five years? Where would it like to be in the next five years?
- How does your company approach change?
- What pending legislation (or market conditions, competitive threats, demographic trends, organizational changes, etc.) could change the way you do business?
- What are the market forces you are most concerned about?
- How is your company addressing the competitive pressures of the market?
- What issues do you think your company must address or overcome in order to be more successful? What specific steps or actions will you need to take?
- Tell me what you'll need to be doing differently to overcome some of the challenges in your market.
- Tell me what's keeping you from dominating your competition.

Questions About Company Culture

"Company culture" can refer to many things, including how the employees feel about the company; what the relationships are between different departments or between headquarters and its subsidiaries; the relationships your contact has with others on her team, with her boss, and with all of the other departments in the company; and how changes are proposed and implemented.

Questions about company culture allow you to become a "fly on the wall" in your customer's boardroom. They give you access to the inner workings of the organization, and help you anticipate problems, obstacles, and objections before they occur.

Company-culture questions are especially useful in three situations.

The first is when you're trying to figure out how your contact fits into the big picture. In this case, the contact's *perception* of the company culture can tell you a lot about how much influence they wield. Do they project a sense of ownership, or do they describe the culture as something external that comes down from the higher-ups, and over which they feel little control? Do people feel valued, empowered, and respected? If your contact sees company culture as something that's imposed on them, versus something they help create, you're probably not talking to a person with a lot of influence.

The second situation is when you're trying to evaluate the quality of the sales opportunity. Unless you're selling a transactional, one-call-and-close product, you're going to be investing time and effort with this organization, and you want to know that your time is well spent. If you're trying to sell into a dysfunctional organization, you'll probably be frustrated. Or if you're selling to a buyer whose values aren't aligned with what you sell—for example, a company that focuses on price when your value proposition is all about long-term value—you need to consider whether this misalignment will lead to a lot of wheel-spinning with not much to show for it. So your questions about culture should be designed to tell you something about the quality of the organization. Do they attract and retain top talent? Is it a place people want to work? Do they take pride in their products? Do they sell on value and not price?

The third area where you want to dig deep into culture is when you're talking to top executives. Their number-one job is to get results through other people, and company culture is one of the tools they use to get their teams pulling in the right direction.

Here are some examples of questions about company culture:

- Tell me how you are trying to create and drive change in order to achieve your goals.
- How would you describe your culture today and how are you looking to enhance it moving forward?
- How would people working for your company describe the atmosphere to outsiders?
- When making a change, how do you introduce it to your employees?
- What plans does your organization have for _____ in the future?
- How do the departments in your company interact?
- Tell me about some of the recent changes in your company's organizational structure.
- How would you describe the relationship between your corporate headquarters and your subsidiaries?
- Which departments (for example, marketing, personnel, or research and development) lead the way in innovation or have a significant impact on the bottom line?
- Is there a single department that makes more of the company's decisions than any other?
- How does your company deal with issues of _____?

Questions About Goals

These questions are designed to assess a buyer's aspirations and desires. Where do they want to go? How fast do they want to grow? What do they want to achieve, improve, enhance, fix, resolve, etc., and by when? These questions will help you find out whether buyers are truly open to change and whether you can help them get there.

Here are some examples:

- Share with me your long-term goals . . . short-term goals.
- Can you prioritize your goals?
- Tell me how your goals align with your (team, department, corporate, etc.) goals.
- Help me understand what's driving you and your team to achieve these goals.
- What concerns do you have if you don't achieve them?
- How do this year's goals differ from last year's goals?
- If you could achieve these goals, what would it mean to you?
- Share with me what you see is the biggest opportunity for you to leverage success.
- Describe your goals to increase market share. What's working well for you? What's not?
- How do you envision success ___ years from now?

Questions About Action Steps

A good way to get clarity on goals is to follow up with questions about what actions will need to occur in order to achieve the goals.

When the prospect can provide clarity to action questions, you know that he or she has given some thought to how the goal will be achieved—which is a strong sign that the buyer is motivated.

The action question is all about, "*How* are you going to achieve this goal?" Think of someone who wants to start an exercise program to get in shape. A goal question would be, "How much weight do you want to lose and by when?" An action question would be, "How are you going to do it?" When the response provides clarity—for example, "I will eliminate saturated and trans fats, restrict my calorie intake to fifteen hundred calories per day, exercise daily for thirty minutes, and get eight hours of sleep per night," you know this person has a good game plan. If the answer is, "Eat less and exercise more," you have to wonder: If they haven't put any energy into designing an action plan, how much energy will they put into actually doing something?

The same goes for prospects. If they haven't identified action steps, they probably won't have much impetus to move forward.

And, by the way, don't be fooled by an answer like this: "You're the expert. You tell me what we have to do." Of course you want to work hard to solve your customers' problems, but they have to work, too. If they don't have some skin in the game, they'll bail the minute things get tough.

Here are some questions you can ask:

- Based on the goals you shared with me, what has to happen to get there?
- What actions will you need to take between now and _____ months from now to achieve your goals?
- What have you tried in the past to achieve this type of goal? What worked, what didn't, and why?
- Share with me what others on your team will need to do in order to achieve these goals.
- What do you anticipate might get in the way, and how will you address this hurdle?
- You have an ambitious goal. Where can you focus your resources to ensure success?
- Tell me what you'll need to do more of . . . less of . . . to achieve the results you're looking for.
- Walk me through the implementation phase.
- How will you measure progress?

The Question of Why

"Why" questions are among the most powerful of all questions. They allow you to understand the motives of your customers—what they want and why they want it. Some customers act out of fear, others out of self-interest, and still others out of a desire to increase profits. Being able to uncover motives brings you invaluable insight into how your customers operate. This knowledge then allows you to provide individualized service for your customers.

Getting information on motives is tricky. If you simply ask, "Why?" over and over again, your customers will probably get annoyed or be offended.

Here are some examples that might help you probe deeper and to better understand what's motivating your customers:

- Tell me, what is prompting your interest in . . . ?
- What's causing this to happen?
- What's driving the need for change?
- What originally led you to this decision?
- Walk me through the steps that led you to this conclusion.
- What do you hope to accomplish?
- Share with me what is motivating your decision to . . . ?
- Why is this important to you?
- What is prompting you to consider taking action?
- What's in it for you to implement this?
- If you can achieve this result, what will it mean to you?
- If you are not able to achieve this result, what concerns do you have? And how might not achieving it personally affect you?

13

Questions About BANT

Budget, Authority, Need, and Timing

MANY YEARS AGO, the big sales brains at IBM came up with a way to evaluate the quality of sales leads. The idea was to establish a short list of questions that every sales rep had to be able to answer—at least tentatively—before a lead could go into their pipeline. These questions focused on four key areas. Leads were considered "validated" if they met at least three of the four criteria.

IBM, being IBM, converted the system into an acronym: BANT. It stands for:

B—Budget. Is there money available? Is it sufficient for whatever solution you're likely to propose?

A—Authority. Does the person or people I'm working with have the power to make a deal happen?

N—Need. Is there an urgent need for what I'm selling?

T—Time frame. Is the buyer ready to move forward immediately? If not, is there an agreed-upon timetable for implementation?

BANT is a deceptively simple concept that has withstood the test of time. In various versions, it's become a key metric that many, if not most, sales organizations use to qualify sales leads. Sometimes it's called ANUM—Authority, Need, Urgency, and Money. Another version is CHAMP—Challenges, Authority, Money, and Prioritization. Others have developed different variants. But the basic idea is the same.

BANT is powerful because it gives salespeople a consistent scorecard, along with a way to structure their questions and gather the information needed for qualifying in one encounter. Nothing is more frustrating than spending time with a prospect and walking away wondering, "Is this a real opportunity or not?" BANT can tell you. If you don't have answers to all four questions, you haven't dug enough.

These questions won't put off real buyers. Many prospects are aware of the concept and know why you're asking. These are widely accepted as legitimate questions that any competent salesperson should be asking. (In fact, if your prospect is unwilling or unable to answer them, that's a pretty strong indication that you're wasting your time.)

That said, you must lay the groundwork first. Imagine if you got a call from a salesperson who asks a few cursory questions about your business and then starts badgering you about your budget, your decisionmaking authority, and so on. You'd end that call pretty quickly. So these questions come after you establish some rapport with a prospect and both of you agree that you'd like to see if there's a basis for doing business together.

Of course, the information you collect at the beginning of the sales process will be tentative and incomplete. For example, buyers may have budget allocated or at least a commitment from management to spend the money. But as company finances change, so do budgets. For that reason, you'll want to return to BANT throughout the sales process to make sure the opportunity remains viable.

You're not looking for certainty. You're looking for commitment. Yes, a budget may change. Authority may shift. Needs may evolve. Timetables may slip. But what you really want to know is whether, at this point in time, you're talking to someone who is willing and able to buy from you.

As you consider BANT, keep in mind that you don't have to address these in the order presented here. In fact, my preferred approach is usually to cover Needs first, followed by Time frame, then Budget, and finally Authority. I find that the conversation flows much more naturally that way. When you start with Needs, it's all about them. You're much more likely to build rapport and get them to open up than if you start the conversation with Budget or Authority. (However, it does make for an awkward acronym: NTBA!)

Need

For the purposes of BANT, "need" is about two things.

The first is urgency. People "need" all sorts of things. What you want to find out is whether there is a need that is sufficiently compelling, at this point in time, to overcome the buyer's inertia and lead to a purchase.

Need is also a way to gain insight into what different people within the decisionmaking process value most, and the criteria they'll be using to assess your proposal. For example, a purchasing agent may need a low price, because it's how he or she is measured. An engineer or IT person, by contrast, may need quality, reliability, and performance. The CEO needs growth, profitability, and increased market share.

You have to determine whether these various stakeholders' needs add up to a sufficiently compelling reason to buy. And you have to determine which needs take precedence. You may not be able to deliver the quality that the engineers want at the price that purchasing demands. So what happens then? Whose needs prevail?

Here are some questions to ask:

- What exactly are your needs?
- Can you prioritize them for me?
- Who's driving this initiative and why?
- What led you to call me/take my call today?
- Tell me what's changed in your organization that's prompting you to address this issue now?
- How will you determine a successful outcome? How will you measure success?
- You mentioned that price, quality, and service were three important criteria. Why those three? Which is most important? Least important?
- Let's assume you are looking at three potential vendors who meet all of your criteria (including price). How would you then make your decision?
- You mentioned that the most important thing for you is price. How does that compare to what others (dealers, end-users, engineering, manufacturing, design, production, marketing, fulfillment) think is most important?
- If you can think back to when you first chose your current product, what were your selection criteria? Based on what you know now, how would those criteria change?
- If you think ahead to three years from now, what do you anticipate will be most important about this purchase? The initial price? The performance over time? The opportunities it opens up for you, your organization, and/or your customers?

- Which characteristics are "must haves" for you, and which are optional?

Time-Frame

Time frame is closely related to Need. If a buyer really, really, really needs something, they'll have a clear timetable for acquiring it. If they say they really need it but are willing to live without it for now, you will be facing an uphill battle. Other priorities are likely to intervene. Meanwhile, your buyer will continue to insist that they really do want to get started, just as soon as this other thing gets squared away.

Timing questions are also closely aligned with questions about Authority. For example, your immediate contact may feel great urgency to get something done. But do the ultimate decisionmakers or other stakeholders feel differently?

Sometimes buyers will be hoping that *you* can light a fire under management when they've been unable to do so themselves. Good luck with that. If the boss is comfortable saying no to your contact, why would she say yes to you, an outsider? When you ask the time-frame question, you find out how committed the organization really is to moving forward.

Here are some examples of time-frame questions:

- How quickly do you want to move forward?
- What's your time frame for getting this done?
- How urgent is this issue? Does it have to be addressed right now, or are there more urgent priorities?
- Do you have a date when you need to get started?
- What might be some roadblocks that could get in the way of getting started by that date?
- Would you say this is a priority? The *top* priority? One of the top three? What's a higher priority?
- Who else sees this/doesn't see this as a priority?
- What happens if you don't get started by . . . ?
- Do you have a schedule or project plan in place? What are the decision points in that plan? Are there dates assigned?

Budget

The "What's your budget?" question is often the most difficult of the BANT questions, so we'll spend more time on it. It can seem intrusive, nosy, or blunt.

And most of the time you get a response like this: "I don't know. Why don't you put together a proposal so that I can present to my team and we'll see where things go?"

In my early days of selling, I would consider that a buying signal and go back to the office to spend hours working up a proposal. I'd submit it, and more often than not one of three things would happen—the first one bad, and the second one worse, and the third one worst of all.

Here's the bad scenario: Things would go silent. I'd never hear from the prospect again. My proposal scared them off, or they never had any interest or money to begin with and didn't want to tell me.

The worse scenario: The prospect reviews my proposal and says, "Wow, that's a lot of money." All of a sudden they become the most educated consumer ever about how much they want to spend. Invariably, their number would be far less than what I'd proposed, or what I was willing to charge. Another wasted effort.

The worst-of-all scenario: The prospect would get back to me with all sorts of questions about the budget. They'd ask me to "sharpen my pencil" and have another go at it. But they still wouldn't tell me whether they had budget allocated. More time invested, same outcome.

So what is my point here? If your time is valuable (and in sales it's all you have), you have to pin the buyer down before you invest more in the opportunity.

Here are examples of respectful, yet direct, ways to get an answer:

You: So I can put together a proposed solution that's going to meet you and your organization's needs, what's your budget?

Prospect: Well, I don't know yet. It's really going to depend on what you propose.

You: I appreciate that. In fact, I face a similar dilemma. I can't create a proposal unless I know how much you can spend. So here's what I suggest: Why don't you find out what your company is prepared to invest? Too often I've seen clients end up spending more money and resources than necessary because they didn't have budget numbers to begin with. So how soon can you get back to me with those numbers?

Here's another approach:

You: I understand and here's what I recommend: Let's find out what budget numbers you have to work with. Because the last thing I want to do is to recommend something that is not in alignment with your goals, needs, and budget expectations. Why put you through that? How soon can you get back to me with some budget numbers?

Some prospects are just shopping around. They really do know what they can spend, or at least have an idea; they just don't want to reveal it. That's not fair to you or to them. How can you help them if they won't tell you what they can spend? I can't tell you how much time and effort I've wasted putting together a quote or proposal and later been told it didn't fit the budget. In other words, there *was* a budget, but someone decided I couldn't be trusted with that information. Not a good way to start a relationship.

That said, there are situations where the prospect is gathering information to help them scope a project. That's a very different situation. It's not a qualified opportunity, so you don't want to spend a lot of time on it. At the same time, it could *become* an opportunity somewhere down the road, so you want to be helpful. The questions might go something like this:

Prospect: Well, we really don't have a budget yet.

You: I see. So let me ask, where are you at in your process? Is this something you're just thinking about? Or are you putting together a budget and need some ballpark figures?

Prospect: Yes, my boss asked me to get some general numbers so we could see if this is something we'd consider.

You: Got it. Of course, since there's a lot more I'd like to know about you and your company, I can't offer any hard-and-fast numbers. But in my experience, companies your size generally allocate somewhere between $ _____ and $ _____ a year. Anything less than that and you probably won't get the impact you need. The high end may be more than you need. But that gives you a range to work with. Does that sound like numbers you could work with?

Prospect: Yes. Would you like to send us a proposal?

You: It sounds like that would be premature until you have a budget approved. Why don't you share these preliminary numbers with your boss, and if this is something you're prepared to invest in, let me know. In fact, the three of us should get together and come up with a proposed plan. What do you think?

What if you are selling basic products such as a tool, a chair, a drill, a forklift, a book, etc., where you don't have to create a proposal? You just look up the product and the price appears. Do you just give the buyer a price?

It depends. In exchange for the information, you can ask a question. You might say, "We have a variety of nice options. So that I can recommend the right one that's going to fit your needs, let me ask you: What budget are you looking to work with?"

Here are additional ways to ask about budgets:

- Share with me the budget parameters you want to stay within.
- What are some budget numbers you're working with?
- Budgetwise, where are you looking to be?
- Walk me through your budgetary approval process.
- How do you go about getting a budget approved for a project like this?
- So what's a low end versus a high end where you need to be in terms of a budget?
- You have told me that your company has allocated $ _____ for this product. How was that amount determined?
- Do you think the allocation of funds is sufficient for the project at hand?
- Can you give me a sense of how much the company is prepared to invest?
- We're not right for everyone. If a company can't invest at least $5,000, we probably can't offer an effective solution. So is that in line with your expectations?

If a prospect won't give you any budget numbers, you can also try feeding them numbers until they respond. It's sort of like poking them with a needle (and how often do you get to do that with prospects?). For example:

You: What's your budget?

Prospect: I don't know.

You: You have a lot of options that might suit your needs, which are in the range of 10 to 40k. Where are you looking to be?

Prospect: Oh, the most we're thinking is around 12 to 15k, max. [Surprise! He did know after all.]

You: So just to make sure I understand, you're thinking your budget is going to be from 12 to 15k. Is that what I am hearing?

Prospect: Yes.

You: And what if you and your organization find the ideal solution that is the perfect fit not just for the short term but for the long term? How much wiggle room do you see beyond 15k?

Prospect: Well, if we found the ideal solution, yes. We'd have some flexibility to go beyond that number

You: And how would you define the ideal solution?

Prospect: If we found a product with long-term durability and no quality or safety concerns, so we don't repeat that costly mistake we had six months ago, then yes, we'd be open to spending more—maybe 20k.

Authority

The next part of BANT is Authority: Who makes the decisions? Who are the champions, naysayers, influencers, and so on?

You won't find out what you need simply by asking your prospect, "Who's the decisionmaker on this?" It's never that simple. Few buyers have absolute authority. Even in the simplest sales—say a couple shopping for a new car—the decisionmaking process is complicated, and it's not always clear who has the final say. In complex sales, that's even more true. In addition, the question comes across as a bit offensive—suggesting that you don't have time for this person unless he or she can buy from you. And it may encourage a prospect to be less than forthright about how much authority he or she really has.

What you're really looking for is a way to *map* the decisionmaking process. You want to know who the players are, how they're going to determine value, and how they interact with one another. You want to know who will have the most influence, who will have the least, and where everybody else falls in between.

Let's face it: Even in the best of worlds, you can't please everybody completely. Not everyone's interests are aligned. Sometimes they're in opposition. You have to know the dynamics or you might be selling to the wrong people or putting forward the wrong value proposition.

Asking about the decisionmaking process is also a way to find out what your prospect values and what they don't. If you ask buyers directly —"What's important to you and your company?"—you're likely to get a lot of vague generalities. When you ask about the decisionmaking process, you get useful and realistic assessments of value. If you can get your customers to express the major criteria that their companies use when making their decisions, you find out what's important to them.

You also need to map the decisionmaking process so you can influence it when the time comes. For example, you may need to maneuver around naysayers and tailor your recommendations to the people who carry the most weight.

And if you can't get a clear picture of the decisionmaking process, that's a strong signal that this may not be an opportunity you want to invest your time in. It could be that you're talking to someone with limited or no authority (which is why they can't tell you how the decision will be made). Or you could be talking to an organization that isn't anywhere close to buying (which is why they haven't established a decisionmaking process).

Here are some authority questions to ask:

- Walk me through your decisionmaking process.
- How are buying decisions made at your company?
- Help me understand your role and who else is involved. Of these people, who's responsible for deciding what?
- As you look at getting approval, who do you see is in favor? Who might oppose it? Of those who might not be in favor, how would you get their buy-in?

- How committed are you to get approval on this project?
- What are the steps that your organization has to take to reach a decision on this type of purchase?
- How do you see the decisionmaking process going?
- Tell me what challenges you foresee in the decisionmaking process.
- Tell me your thoughts on this upcoming project. How does your boss feel about it? Your peers? Others on your team? The committee?
- How can we tailor this message so everyone sees it as a win instead of a loss?
- Share with me your personal interest in the successful outcome of this project.

14

For Future Sales, Ask About the Past

DURING EVERY SALES training session, I ask salespeople to write down the questions they ask on a regular basis, whether in a first-time sales call or when renewing an established relationship.

Without fail, about 90 percent of the questions we tally are about the present. For example:

- What are you currently doing?
- How many are you producing?
- How do you use this product/application?
- What vendor are you using?
- What do you like about them?
- Are you the decisionmaker?
- What are your biggest challenges?
- What can I do for you?

Only a few questions are about the future, and rarely do I collect *any* about the past. If there is a question about the past, it's usually a warm-up question, such as, "How long have you been with the company?"

Why don't salespeople ask questions about the past? Some think that dwelling on what happened last year, or even last month, is irrelevant. Salespeople have told me: "I can only make money in the present or the future. The past is dead, done, and gone. So why bother asking questions about it?"

Here's why: because the customer's *present* problems and *future* responses are rooted in the past.

Asking questions about the past is a wonderful way to understand your customers' priorities, motives, and behaviors. Imagine that you are interviewing a prospective employee. You wouldn't focus all of your questioning on the present or the future. You would want to know what the candidate had accomplished in the past and how she had made her choices. The reason you ask these questions is because they will help you understand what the candidate is likely to do if you hire her.

It's exactly the same when you're talking to prospects and customers.

Questions about the past allow you to discover how you can best sell to customers in the future. They also help you understand how they think and act. For example, they allow you to understand the nature and magnitude of problems the customer has encountered, how the customer responded, and the outcomes he experienced. You learn which players were involved. You gain insights into their former or current vendor relationships and the strength of those relationships. You learn about organizational changes, trends, or competitive threats they have weathered.

In fact, nearly everything you need to know about a customer can be found in the past. So why not spend more time there?

Here are some examples of questions you can ask about the past:

- What would you say is different about your organization today from when you started with this company?
- What originally led you to work for this company? What were your expectations when you came on board, and how have they changed since you've been here?
- Since you have been with the company, what have been some of the biggest hurdles you have faced?
- Could you tell me about the changes your department has gone through recently? What challenges or opportunities did those changes create for you?
- As you look back on your career, what has given you the greatest sense of accomplishment? If you could do it over again, what would you do differently?
- What could others learn from your experiences?
- Tell me about your relationships with vendors in the past—your current ones and the ones you no longer do business with.

- Can you give me an example of a significant problem you faced in the past when dealing with _____ and how you responded to it?
- What trends in the market have you seen over the past few years?
- What steps did your organization have to take to adapt to this trend?
- Think back to when you originally implemented this process. What were your expectations? What results are you getting now? What kind of results would you like to get in the future?

When you ask questions like these, something interesting happens with customers. They think bigger. When you focus exclusively on the present, your customer will almost inevitably fixate on their day-to-day struggles. And while these problems may seem urgent to the buyer, the value you provide by fixing them tends to be as fleeting and transitory as the problems themselves.

When you ask buyers to look back, you're asking them to take a longer view. They can see that perhaps that seemingly minor problem they're grappling with today—"It took me all morning to create these reports!"—is just a symptom of a deeper, systemic problem. If you can address that larger problem instead of just the immediate pain, you can deliver much greater value.

For example, you ask the customer, "How long have you been struggling to create these reports? And why?"

The customer replies: "It's been every month for the past two years. As our business got larger, we found that our quarterly projections were off the mark. Our CEO had a very awkward exchange with shareholders, and after that he insisted that we do real-time reporting."

Consider how rich a history like that can be for a salesperson. The customer's day-to-day problem is how to get those reports out on time. When you get the buyer focused on a longer time horizon, the problem is revealed to be much deeper—how to deliver reliable data to meet the needs of senior management and shareholders.

That's a much larger opportunity to pursue. And a much more valuable one for you. As a mentor of mine once said, "Where there's a past, there's a P.O."

15

Getting to Yes Without All the Stress

Anxiety-Free Closing Questions

IN AN IDEAL world, closing a sale is a nonevent. You deeply understand the buyer's needs. You know how much they can spend. You've identified all of the stakeholders and addressed any concerns they may have. You know how the buying decision will be made. Through careful questioning, you've helped your buyer see what's at stake and the consequences of inaction or delay. Budget questions have been asked and answered. The value proposition is solid. Asking for the order is a mere formality.

In the real world, of course, things don't always go as smoothly. Perhaps the buyer has been less than forthcoming despite your best efforts. Maybe a hidden influencer is waiting in the wings. Maybe the buyer doesn't really understand how your solution creates value—or doesn't agree with your analysis. Maybe new information has surfaced that changes the situation, and the buyer hasn't shared it with you.

Even when you've done all you can, there's always some degree of risk when you get to the close. The questioning techniques I've described in this book are designed to reduce the unknowns to a minimum. But there are no guarantees. I've even seen—as I'm sure you have—"closed" sales that later get unclosed. You never really know whether you have the sale until the check clears.

Understandably, that "unknown" factor creates anxiety in salespeople. They've put so much time and work into the sale. They need it to hit their numbers. Now the moment of truth has arrived, and they're either going to win or lose. Given the stakes, confident salespeople can turn into shrinking violets. They dance around the issue. They hem and haw. That lack of confidence can be infectious. A buyer who'd been fully prepared to say yes starts to get second thoughts.

The real source of that anxiety, I believe, is how salespeople look at closing. In most cases, closing is *not* an either/or situation. You want your buyer to say yes, of course. But in many cases, a "no" isn't the end of the road. It means you have more work to do.

Many of the old-school manipulative closing questions—which I *don't* endorse—are based on this either/or view of closing. They try to use psychological tricks to boost the odds of getting a yes—as if, somehow, you can distract or fool an otherwise reluctant buyer into saying yes. But in my experience, buyers see closing questions like "Would you prefer the red one or the blue one?" or "Will that be cash or charge?" for what they are: pushy tactics. And by eroding the buyer's trust, they move you *further* away from a yes. We want buyers to say yes because they really want to buy, not because they got fast-talked.

That being said, some buyers do need a little nudge to say yes. Not because the deal isn't good for them, but because they're feeling some anxiety about making a decision. The thing about anxiety is that it's contagious: A buyer's anxiety can make you anxious, which, in turn, can add to the buyer's anxiety.

That's why asking the right questions is so important. Information is power. When you understand your prospect's needs, your solution is on target, specific, and meaningful. And if the buyer needs a little push, you can do so confidently, knowing that it really is in the customer's best interest to embrace that solution. Buyers know, too, and chances are they'll respect you for helping them move forward.

Here's my other problem with traditional closing questions: The term "closing" itself puts too much attention on the last steps of a sale. I prefer to use terms such as "getting a commitment" or "agreeing to the next step." In that sense, *every* interaction with a buyer needs to be "closed." You need to secure a next step, whether it's saying yes to the sale, setting up the next appointment, agreeing to introduce you to other decisionmakers, arranging a demonstration, or some other call to action.

At every stage, the greatest risk you face isn't getting a "no" decision from the buyer; it's getting "no decision" from the buyer. A "yes" is best, but a "no" is at least liberating. It allows you to move on to better opportunities. When you don't insist on a decision, you end up wasting huge amounts of time on opportunities that will drift along and end up going nowhere.

So with those thoughts in mind, let's look at some questions that can help you navigate the close, increase the odds of getting a yes, and continue the dialogue if the buyer says no.

When to Transition to the Close

Salespeople often ask me, "When is it time to transition to closing?"

My reply: Don't ask me. Ask your customer.

You'll recall that impact questions are a great way to size up an opportunity. The customer's response will tell you which stage they're in:

- The "have to" stage (the consequences of not moving forward right away will have serious ramifications)
- The "want to" stage (motivated to do something, but not ready to act yet)
- The "should" stage (no real desire)

Buyers in the "have to" stage are ready to buy. Don't waste time beating around the bush, or they may buy from someone else to get immediate relief.

Buyers in the "want to" are motivated and interested. You should try to close them, if only to see how serious they are.

However, you're going to hear some version of "Yes, but." For example, "I'm really interested but I have to run this by some other people." Or, "I'd like to move forward but first I have to get budget approval." Or, "Yes, this problem is costing us money, but first we have to fix. . . ." Or, "Yes, I've told my boss how serious this situation is, but I can't seem to get through to her."

People don't buy in the "want to" stage—they procrastinate due to fears, doubts, lack of money, lack of authority, conflicting priorities, or timing issues. But that doesn't mean you should abandon them. Your number-one job is to identify the objections and agendas (which may be hidden) and resolve them so you can move the buyer to the "have to" stage, where they clearly recognize the need for change outweighs any desire to stay put.

With buyers in the "should" stage, it's obviously too soon to start closing. You'll either get a brush-off or a buyer who pretends to be interested (either out of politeness or to get more information from you). But even though buyers in this stage aren't ready to be "closed," you can and should be asking for a next step. For example:

Salesperson: So it sounds like this is something that your management is thinking about, right?

Buyer: Well, yes, they're thinking about it. But I don't think it's a priority right now.

Salesperson: And why is that?

Buyer: We're in the middle of a systems upgrade right now. Until we get that done, we can't really focus on this issue.

Salesperson: When do you think you'll get that done?

Buyer: It's supposed to be done by the end of the year.

Salesperson: Assuming that happens, do you think what we discussed will then become a priority?

Buyer: I don't know. Give me a call then and we'll figure it out.

Salesperson: Okay. Can we set up a call for 10:00 a.m. on January 6?

Buyer: Well, it's too far out to put on my calendar but give me a call in December and we can talk about where we are for next year.

With this approach, you've efficiently achieved two things: (1) You've avoided wasting time on an opportunity that's not yet ripe and may never be ripe—for example, by spending time trying to "educate" the buyer or trying to create urgency. And (2) you've asked for and received a commitment to a next step. Granted, the buyer's commitment is low—he won't agree to a time and date, which indicates that the chances of making any progress in December will be minimal. But at least he's agreed to a phone call to reconnect.

Another way to know whether it's time to close is by using opinion questions. As you move through the sales process, ask your buyer what they're thinking.

In my experience, salespeople too often skip this simple but important step. For example, how many times have you sat in on a Power-Point presentation and the salesperson simply plows on to the end, only to find that his or her listeners checked out somewhere along the way? Great sales presenters will stop at key points and ask, "So what are your thoughts? Could you see this working for you? How so?" Or, "Does this look like what you had in mind so far?" Or, "Before this goes further, let me ask how this pertains to what you're dealing with."

So why do many salespeople overlook these basic questions? They're too focused on getting through their sales pitch. Or they fear they'll open up the can of worms. Or they don't have a Plan B if the buyer says the presentation is off base or starts asking questions that could cause the salesperson to lose control of the presentation.

But this simple technique is incredibly powerful. When you take your buyer's pulse throughout the sales process, it keeps buyers engaged, shows you are attentive to their needs, and allows you to shift gears so that you stay aligned with what the buyer is thinking.

Asking for the Order

It will come as no surprise to you that I don't believe in "magic questions" when it's time to ask for the order. A simple, confident, and conversational approach is best:

"So what do you say?"

"How soon would you like to get started?"

"Should we go ahead and finalize the paperwork?"

" I recommend that you go ahead and approve it today so we can get this set up by _____ and you can start realizing the benefits right away. How's that sound?"

"So that you can get the most from _____ , I suggest we _____ . Does that work for you?"

You want to convey to your buyer that this is just the next step in a natural process. You don't want to create anxiety by overselling the close, but at the same time you want to be perfectly clear that you're asking for a decision.

Some salespeople try to soften the close by phrasing it as an opinion question. As I've said, an opinion question is a great tool for moving *toward* the close, but not when you're *asking* for the business. As a rule of thumb, consider asking at least two opinion questions and if you get positive responses, ask for a decision. For example:

Salesperson: Is this what you had in mind?

Prospect: Yes.

Salesperson: How do you think your boss will feel about it?

Prospect: Oh, he'll really like it.

Salesperson: Okay, then. Why don't we go ahead and get the paperwork approved so we can get started?

Wait for It

Once you've presented the proposal and price, remain silent and wait for the buyer's response. Silence gives a customer an opportunity to reflect.

Silence can make salespeople extremely uncomfortable. In fact, for some salespeople, closing is the one and only time they shut up.

Think about that for a moment. In that silence, the customer's mind is fully engaged as they work out their decision. They don't have to think nearly as hard when you're talking. So why limit that powerful process to the last moments of the sale? The more silence you can build into your sales conversations, the more engagement and better thinking you get from prospects. Imagine how much more business you could get!

If the Answer is No

So what if the buyer says no?

Assuming you've gotten this far—you've properly qualified the buyer, worked hard to understand their needs, and presented what you believe to be a good value proposition—you've earned the right to ask the buyer why. Not so you can argue with him or her, but so you can understand what you missed. As long as the buyer is willing to engage in a good-faith dialogue, a "no" isn't the end of the road. It's an opportunity for you to gather more information so that you can propose the right solution.

The conversation might go something like this:

Buyer: I'm sorry. I just don't think this is going to work for us.

Salesperson: Well, of course I'm sorry to hear that. And, to be honest, surprised. I thought I'd addressed the needs you'd expressed. So help me understand what I missed.

Buyer: Well, I'm just not convinced that we'll actually see the results you're promising here. I know you believe you can deliver on them, but if we spend all this money and this doesn't work, heads will roll, including mine.

That isn't all bad news. When buyers give you an unexpected no, they're really telling you that you didn't do your due diligence earlier. The buyer has just revealed to you—perhaps for the first time—what's really at stake for him personally.

That's incredibly powerful knowledge—but it means that you do have to take a step back and explore this issue. Often you'll feel tempted to push forward—you were so close to getting the sale!—but the more you try to gloss over the issues, the more anxiety the buyer will feel.

Instead, take a deep breath, slow down, and take one step back: You might say: "I understand your concerns and I want to see if we can address them. Can you help me understand why you think this might not work?"

You may be able to address the buyer's concerns then and there, or you may have to ask for some more time. For example, you might say, "We both understand that there are no absolute guarantees. At the same time, you've acknowledged that your current situation isn't sustainable. Would it be helpful for you to talk to some of my other clients to learn how they made the program successful?" Or, "Why don't we go ahead with a pilot so you and your team can realize the benefits firsthand? We'll even back it up with a thirty-day satisfaction guarantee, which will minimize the risk and investment on your end."

It's disappointing to have to back up when you thought you had a deal, but don't panic. Flush out the concerns. Get them out on the table. Let the prospect talk. In many ways it's therapeutic to allow them to verbalize their concerns, so they can come to the right conclusion—which of course is to move forward, all based on your questions.

CHAPTER

16

Upselling and Cross-Selling Questions

Stop Leaving Money on the Table and Get Your Full Share
of the Customer's Business

CONSIDER THIS REAL-LIFE scenario:

I was consulting with a tire wholesaler, which worked with agricultural equipment dealers. These dealers have a lot of inventory sitting on their lots. One way to move that inventory is to configure it to meet the needs of a specific buyer. For example, a farmer may grow alfalfa, but the dealer has a tractor that's set up for corn farming. By switching out the wheel sets—a relatively inexpensive modification—the dealer can set up the tractor for alfalfa and close a sale.

New wheel sets require new wheels—and in a hurry. So when the dealer calls the tire wholesaler, the salesperson jumps on the order. It's a quick and lucrative sale. The salesperson is happy. The dealer is happy. The farmer is happy.

Everybody's happy. Maybe a little too happy—because a huge opportunity was missed.

I worked with the distributor's sales force to turn these calls into upselling opportunities. Instead of simply taking the order, I urged salespeople to ask a series of follow-up questions. For example:

"Hey, Bob. While I have you on the phone, tell me about some of the other hard-to-move equipment sitting on your lot right now. How long has it been sitting? What's it costing you in terms of financing charges, overhead, etc.?

"Also, what kind of equipment are you seeing a high demand for? If you could fit out this equipment with different wheel sets, do you think you could meet that demand and move more stuff off your lot?

"And, by the way, who else at the dealership is facing this problem?"

Asking questions like these unleashed a torrent of additional business. Bob might be working on one deal, but there are likely to be seven other Bobs at the dealership who are trying to move other pieces of hard-to-sell equipment. And there might be three other branches across the state. By asking for an upsell, a single easy sale becomes a huge opportunity.

There are just two ways to get a sale: (1) finding new customers and selling something to them, and (2) selling something new to existing customers.

Of course, the first is necessary if you want sales to grow in the long term. But selling to existing customers is more efficient. Yet in my experience, it often gets less attention from salespeople than it should. Yes, there is something exhilarating about bringing a new buyer aboard. But if you don't make the most of existing opportunities, you won't get the best return on your time and effort.

Upselling and cross-selling leverage the work you've already done. (To clarify our terms: In this chapter I refer to "upselling" as selling other goods and services to the same buyer. "Cross-selling" involves selling to another buyer in the same organization.) Buyers know you and understand how you add value. And you know the buyers. All of that knowledge you've so painstakingly acquired serves as the foundation for a new sale.

These opportunities are extraordinarily valuable for another reason as well: *The buyer has already made a decision to do business with you.* And that's the biggest decision that any buyer must make: Do I believe in this salesperson? Is she willing and able to help me?

What's more, buyers have an emotional and psychological investment in buying from you again, because it validates their *previous* decision to buy from you. Nobody wants to think he made a mistake. That's why the best time to explore cross-selling and upselling opportunities is *right after you've closed a sale.* Your buyer's perception of you is at an all-time high.

So why do salespeople often fail to make the most of upselling and cross-selling opportunities? The primary reason, I believe, is because they don't have a plan. All of their thinking and energy is focused on getting that original sale. When they hear that "yes," they feel a huge sense of relief and elation. They've just scored a win, and they want to enjoy it.

The other reason salespeople hold back is because they don't want to push their luck. They believe it's better to get a few crumbs than nothing. Or they don't want to come across as greedy or ungrateful. That's a valid concern—a clumsy attempt can tarnish your reputation with a customer and make them leery about buying from you again.

On the other hand, if you asked great questions to explore the customer's problems and identify what it's costing in terms of time, resources, and opportunities, and you have a solution that will not only alleviate their problems but get them to their goals sooner, you're not being greedy or pushy. If you truly believe you can create more value for the customer, you have an obligation to explore an upsell or cross-sell opportunity. One of the best benefits of cross-selling and upselling is that you position yourself as a partner to your customer, not simply an order taker. Smart buyers will see that you're thinking one step ahead and helping them get ahead of problems instead of simply reacting to them.

Laying the Groundwork

It's critically important to plan your upsell and cross-sell strategy ahead of time. Think of upselling and cross-selling as an integral part of the original sale, not as an extra tacked on to the end if you happen to remember. And start working on them early—during your initial sales discovery.

As with any aspect of sales, your success at upselling and cross-selling depends on the quality of the information you collect. And the quality of the information depends on the quality of the questions you ask.

Here's an example of a low-quality questioning technique: Your customer has just agreed to order five hundred units of whatever it is you sell. You say, "You know, if you could increase that quantity to a thousand units, I can offer you a discount." Or, "We've got a special this month on ____ . Would you be interested in placing an order?" Or, "Do you think any other divisions of your company would be interested in talking to me?"

Questions like these demonstrate no effort or insight. They're simply a slightly more professional version of "Would you like fries with that?" Even worse, they're all about you and what you want. They're not connected to a buyer's need, want, or problem. If the buyer needed one thousandunits, she would have said so, and a discount on units she doesn't need is no bargain. (And even if she does agree to the one thousand units, your selling tactic is forcing you to give up hard-earned margins that you and your company need to remain profitable.) Suggesting that she order an extra five hundred units "just in case" sends a message that you might not be reliable. Fishing around for another division tells the buyer that you don't understand their organization.

Effective upsells and cross-sells use the same types of questions we've discussed earlier—lock-on questions, impact questions, comparison questions, and so on. The time to ask them is during your initial sales discovery process. That's when your buyer is eager to help you understand their needs and learn about their organization, so the questions don't seem pushy or unnatural at all.

For example, here's how you might identify an upselling opportunity using lock-on, comparison, and impact questions:

Buyer: We really need to get a handle on our travel. Last year, my department exceeded the travel budget by 20 percent—mostly because we booked flights at the last minute.

Salesperson: That's quite a lot. I'm sure you could find better uses for that money. You mentioned last-minute flights. Is that an issue that's unique to your department, or do others in your company struggle with it, too?

Buyer: Oh, we've talked about it a lot. It's a widespread problem.

Salesperson: If you could help other departments solve this issue, how big an impact might that have, companywide?

Buyer: It probably adds up to hundreds of thousands of dollars across the entire company.

Salesperson: And what would that mean for you?

Buyer: If I could save our company hundreds of thousands of dollars? It wouldn't hurt my career, that's for sure.

And here's how you might uncover an upselling opportunity using an expansion question:

Buyer: We're interested in five hundred units of Product X.

Salesperson: Great. While I'm pulling up that information, tell me how you arrived at that amount and what you're hoping to accomplish.

As you can see, questions like these don't seem pushy or aggressive. At this stage of the sale, you're simply gathering information. You may find that your buyer's department really is the only one that uses Product

X, or that the buyer has a good reason for ordering five hundred units. Or you may find that other departments are looking to save money, too, or that the buyer hasn't really given much thought to how many units they'll actually need.

Notice, too, that questions like these are all about adding value. You want to ask a series of questions that are focused on how you can help the buyer with additional needs, not how you can get more money from them. Specifically, you want to ask questions that identify other needs in the buyer's organization and questions that help establish a personal benefit to the buyer.

A Question of Timing

The timing of an upsell or cross-sell depends on your customer. You have to know your buyer.

For any number of reasons, your buyer may only be interested in solving *his* immediate problem. He may be risk averse; he may have limited authority or influence. He may not be interested in considering a bigger picture. So does that mean you don't have an upselling or cross-selling opportunity? Not at all! It simply means you need to solve this buyer's immediate need *first*. Get the business—and *then* ask for the upsell or cross-sell.

On the other hand, if your buyer thinks in broader terms, she may see the upsell or a cross-sell as a way to deliver additional value, personally and to her organization. "If I can help reduce travel costs across the board, I'll be a hero around here," she may think. Or, "If I can analyze our needs and find out how many units we *really* should be ordering, my boss will see that I'm more than an order taker." Or, "If I can hit my performance metrics this year, I'll be first in line for a management position."

In such situations, asking about the upsell or cross-sell early may actually help you close the sale. You're helping the buyer solve problems—and delivering more value—while your competitors are just taking orders.

How to Ask

Since you've now gathered the information you need to create a compelling value proposition, asking for the upsell or cross-sell is relatively

straightforward. But don't try to wing it. Decide when and how you're
going to ask.

Here are step-by-step methods you can follow:

Asking for an Upsell

1. **Reestablish value.** For example: "Let's go back to what originally
    led you to choose the solution you went with. How's it meeting
    your needs so far?" Or, "How do you see this program benefiting
    you and your organization?"
2. **Revisit needs.** "When we first spoke, you also mentioned some
    other issues, such as _____ . Tell me, is that still something you
    want to address?" Or, "As we were working on this solution, I also
    noticed _____ . Is that an issue?"
3. **Use vision questions to encourage buyers to think more
    broadly.** "Now that you have a better way to track employee per-
    formance, what are your thoughts about leveraging that data to
    improve your business?" Or, "This program will increase your
    bottom line by 3 percent. What if we could get that number up to
    5 percent?"
4. **Ask permission.** "May I share with you some other ideas that
    might get us there?"

Asking for a Cross-Sell

1. **Reestablish value.** See above.
2. **Be specific.** "Earlier, you mentioned that Joe, your counterpart in
    the Dallas plant, uses a similar production system. Do you think
    this program might be of interest to Joe as well? . . . Tell me more
    about his needs."
3. **Ask for the next step.** "Would you be willing to introduce me
    to . . . ?" "Who else should I talk to at . . . ?"

17

Relationship-Building Questions

Creating Intimacy and Trust

WHEN YOU SELL, what are you selling? A product? A service? A program?

If you think your job is to sell "stuff," you are an endangered species. Nobody needs you. Not your customer, who can buy stuff all day long with the click of a mouse button. Not your employer, who would love to get their stuff in the hands of customers without paying for a very expensive salesperson.

Are you selling "solutions"? The Internet is bursting at the seams with how-to articles, videos, and tutorials in which experts are willing to solve your customer's problems for free.

Are you selling "value"? You'd better hurry up. The easiest way for a customer to "add value" is by shopping around and finding someone who's willing to sell what you sell for 10 percent less.

In the final analysis, you really have only one thing to sell: yourself. You are the one thing that can't be commodified or undercut. Buyers must be confident that by doing business with *you*, they will experience more success, more satisfaction, and less risk than with anyone else. They must trust you.

In the opening chapter of this book, I defined a question as a "truth-seeking missile." Remember that, as humans, we're deeply conditioned to answer a question, as long as it's asked with worthy intent. And when we answer questions, we show our true selves—sometimes more than we even realize.

Curiously, trust begins when buyers reveal themselves to *you*, not the other way around. That's why questions are so important to building a relationship. They encourage buyers to reveal themselves.

When it comes to trust, all of us are faced with two conflicting emotions: On the one hand, we have a deep need to be understood. At the same time, we're careful about disclosing vulnerabilities, because we worry that they'll be used against us. When you ask empathetic and insightful questions, you signal that you truly do want to understand the buyer, and that you have their best interests at heart.

So let's look at how you can structure relationship-building questions at different stages in the sales process.

Building New Relationships

Salespeople tend to be problem-solvers. The minute they see a customer with a problem, they want to roll up their sleeves and get to work on it.

But you can't hurry trust. You can't manipulate a business relationship into *your* specific time frame. And you can't solve a customer's problem until you've been given permission to do so.

So put your solutions away. Take a deep breath, slow down, and invest time in the relationship-forming process by asking the right questions about the customer's past, present, and future.

Are there exceptions? Of course. If a customer is ready to place an order or a crisis falls on your lap where the customer needs your solution pronto, you sell & close the opportunity. But for all those other situations where you have to put time and effort into the sale, focus on building the relationship.

Equally important, *listen* to the answers. I can't tell you how many times I've seen salespeople approach relationship-building questions as a necessary task that they want to get through as quickly as possible so they can get to the "real" job of selling something. I've listened to countless calls where the salesperson reels off a canned list of "relationship-building" questions—some of which may actually be very good—and then drops the ball when the customer actually responds with something significant. Instead of following up, the salesperson just keeps plowing forward.

Think about how that looks from the customer's perspective. He or she has taken a risk by revealing a need or even a vulnerability. Then it becomes obvious that the person asking the question doesn't really care. Is that someone worthy of their trust?

Warm-Up Questions

Another problem I see is that many salespeople are afraid to ask a meaningful question—especially in an initial sales conversation—because it feels emotionally risky. So they never go beyond safe, superficial questions about the weather, sports, the weekend, or what's happening in the news.

There's nothing wrong with asking a few icebreaker questions. It's a social ritual. But these kinds of questions don't build value. So after you've gotten them out of the way, go ahead and ask some questions that help you gain insight on what your prospects are experiencing on the job and the challenges they and their organizations are facing. The responses may reveal valuable information about the organization and how best to position your solutions (not immediately, but later on when the time is right).

Of course, you don't want to pepper new prospects with questions that feel like a cross-examination. The idea is to start a conversational thread that resonates with the buyer and gets them to open up a little. For example:

Salesperson: So I see you're in charge of reviewing client contracts for your firm. How long have you been doing that?

Prospect: Oh, for about the past year.

Salesperson: So what would you say has surprised you most in the past year?

Prospect: Hmmm. I guess I was surprised by how many people in the organization think contracts are just routine. I used to think that myself.

Salesperson: But now you don't?

Prospect: No. Every contract is different. It takes a lot more time than I'd imagined.

At this point, you might be tempted to start solving this "problem." Resist the temptation. Instead, just make a note of what the buyer told you so you can come back to it later. Your goal for now is to show empathy and insight.

Salesperson: I can imagine. I think most people just don't understand how complicated these contracts can get.

Prospect: You're telling me.

As you can see in this example, the initial question is very general and easy for the customer to answer. And it's nonthreatening. There's very little risk involved in telling someone how long you've been doing the job. Each follow-up question flows naturally from what the prospect has already revealed, but digs a little deeper.

In some cases, of course, a buyer's responses will be more guarded than in this example. But it's often surprising how quickly buyers will open up. In fact, some seem like they've been waiting all day for you to ask. After all, how often do they encounter someone who's genuinely interested in what they do?

Here are some other questions you can use to get the ball rolling:

- So tell me what you like most about _____ ? What do you like least about it?
- What would you say is different about your organization (project, job, etc.) today since you started?
- Could you share with me some past experiences with vendors when it comes to _____ .?
- How are you dealing with [name a current industry issue or problem]?
- What originally led you to take on this responsibility/project/job/ task, etc.?
- What were your expectations when you started, and how have they changed as you look at your needs today?

Evaluating Established Relationships

It's all too easy for salespeople to take relationships with their customers for granted. You may think you have a solid relationship—in fact, the customer may tell you so. But there will always be others in the organization who have their own favorite suppliers, or who would like to redeploy your budget toward their pet projects. And other suppliers are constantly knocking at the door, looking for a way in. The reality is that if your customer relationship isn't moving forward, it will sooner or later start moving backward.

In my experience, salespeople often overestimate the quality of these relationships. They assume that if the customer has been buying from them for a long time, hasn't voiced any complaints, and continues to place orders, then the relationship is fundamentally solid. Then, boom—the rug gets pulled out from under them. Without warning, the buyer announces that they're looking at other vendors to save money (or, even worse, that they've already decided to switch). Or the company is being acquired, or a key contact has been replaced, and the new bosses have their own preferred vendors. Or suddenly the buyer lays out a long list of concerns about shipments, delays, quality, lack of new ideas, poor responsiveness, or whatever.

Salespeople often feel betrayed and blindsided, but in most cases they've created the situation. They failed to be proactive about the status of the relationship. Either they were too afraid to ask, or they assumed that the customer would raise any concerns in a fair and timely manner.

But look at it from the customer's perspective: It's not *their* job to work on *your* relationship. Like everyone, they want to avoid conflict and drama. Or they worry that if they give you a heads up that they're looking at other vendors, you won't give them their money's worth.

If you wait for your customers to determine the status of your relationship, you risk hearing about it after they have taken their business elsewhere. Instead, be proactive and monitor your customers by asking them these questions:

- What is it that you value most about doing business with us [me]?
- In what ways are we [am I] helping you to achieve your goals?
- How can we create more value for you and your organization?
- In what ways can we [I] improve?
- What changes do we [I] need to make to ensure greater success?
- If you could change one thing about our relationship, what would it be?
- What goals would you like to see us [me] accomplish with you in the next twelve months?
- Would you be willing to serve as a reference for my product or company? If so, can you elaborate on what you would say about us? If not, why not?
- What will it take on our [my] part to win the business you are giving to our competition?

Many salespeople avoid these kinds of questions. Why? Because they are afraid of the answers. After all, what if customers respond that they are not satisfied? What if they want faster turnarounds, greater discounts, and higher quality? How do you respond?

You respond with gratitude and a desire to meet those requests by asking for things in return.

What if your customer wants better pricing? You get him to commit to purchasing greater volume. If your customer wants faster turnaround, price those projects at a premium so that they get the extra attention, commitment, and support that the customer values. Relationships are always two-sided, so do not be afraid to ask what you can do to enhance the relationship while asking for something in return.

What if you already know your service or quality is poor? Then there is no need to ask these questions. Instead, fix the problem first, then ask whether the fix was successful. (If you fail to ask, your competition will surely do it for you!)

Questions to Elevate the Relationship

Even if your customer relationship is solid, can you make it better?

About once or twice a year, I enjoy taking my important clients to lunch or dinner so we can reflect on our recent accomplishments working together. My other objective is to explore how our business relationship can improve and how I can add more value in the months (or year) ahead. These questions are asked in a relaxed atmosphere and when there's time to talk about the big picture.

Here are some questions you can ask in such a setting. Keep in mind that these aren't "selling" questions in the classic sense. The tone should be one of celebrating shared successes. Be sure to put them into your own words so the questions are conversational. And of course, continue with lots of follow-up questions:

- What do you feel we are/I am doing right to sustain our business relationship?
- What could we be doing differently (more of/less of . . . or where can we improve) in order to ensure that you achieve your upcoming goals?

- What's the most important thing you'd like us to know so that we can stay aligned with your objectives?
- If we could do one thing to enhance our business relationship, what might that be?
- Are we doing anything that makes your job harder? And what can we be doing to make your job easier? More rewarding? To make your company more profitable? To make you more successful?
- If a prospective customer were to ask you to explain why you do business with us, how would you respond?

It may seem risky to open up a conversation with a buyer about where you could be doing a better job. For example, the buyer says, "We really like your quality. But one area we think you could improve is your on-site support."

Your first reaction might be to think you've just stirred up a hornet's nest. Now you'll have to give up more margin and deliver more resources to keep the customer happy. I don't see it that way at all. The customer has just told you that they want something more. Why assume that they're not willing to give anything in return? Maybe they'll pay more, or commit to giving you more business. A relationship is two-sided. So you might reply:

"We can absolutely give you more on-site support. Let me give that some thought, and I'll put together a proposal that will address your needs."

18

Accountability Questions

Hold Buyers' Feet to the Fire—and Have Them Love You for It

BUYERS DEMAND ACCOUNTABILITY from sellers. They expect you to honor your word, deliver what you promised, disclose any potential drawbacks to your product, warn you about problems, and generally tell the truth.

Salespeople often don't hold buyers to the same standard. "The customer is always right," they think. "He who pays the piper calls the tune." They assume that as long as buyers sign the check, we have no right to expect anything further from them.

I disagree.

For one thing, buyers aren't giving you money out of charity or the goodness of their hearts. They're getting something of value in exchange. In a healthy business relationship, both sides have the right, and obligation, to set expectations for the other party.

Even more important, buyers *need* you to establish mutual expectations—what *you're* going to be accountable for and what you expect the *buyer* to be accountable for.

Smart buyers will insist on this clarity for a very simple reason: They don't want to fail.

Let's say you've tried, unsuccessfully, to lose weight using diet books, a gym membership, or some kind of fitness app. Now you've decided to join Weight Watchers or a similar program.

You've taken this step—and plunked down a good bit of money—for one reason: accountability. These programs *share* accountability with you. Yes, they promise to do certain things. But the reason they're successful—and why you're willing to pay a premium for their services—is because they hold *you* accountable. They're designed in a way that doesn't let you off the hook.

You make your goals public to your peers and family. You go every week to get weighed in, in front of everyone. The scale doesn't lie, and your weight is recorded. If you start to slip, you expect someone to call and say, "Hey, we haven't seen you. Where have you been?"

And if you tell them, well, you've been busy at work and there were some family parties, and you've been under a lot of stress, what do you want them to say? "No problem. Take your time. We'll keep taking money out of your checking account, so whenever you're ready to come back, feel free to do so"?

No. You want them to keep you on track to success. You want them to ignore your excuses and say, "We expect to see you this Wednesday at six. Will you commit to that?"

You're fine with a little tough love, because you know that both of you share the same goal. In the long run, the only way they win is if their clients actually lose weight. So for their own selfish reasons, they want to see you win.

It's the same idea when you hire a personal trainer at the gym. You don't want somebody to coddle you. You don't want to hear, "I can't believe how well you're doing" when both of you know you haven't made any progress. You're paying for results, so you want them to challenge you—lift more weight, do more reps, run faster, work harder.

That's what your buyers want, too. They're not buying a friend. They're not buying a cheerleading section. They're buying success. And they want—in fact, *demand*—that you help them get there. Part of your job is to make sure they do their job. Salespeople can absolutely push their customers if they truly have their customers' best interests at heart.

I've seen many salespeople who put relationships ahead of success. Their company tells them to meet with the customer every month, so they "stop by" to see how things are going or call the customer to "check in." They shoot the breeze a bit, ask a few cursory questions, perhaps pick up the tab for lunch. But they don't do anything to ensure success—which means that these time-consuming and sometimes expensive encounters create no value for the seller or the buyer.

If you're selling complex, long time-frame solutions, that approach courts disaster. There's a lot that can go wrong if you don't stay on top of things. And when the chips are down, I've yet to meet a buyer who says, "No worries. Even though we failed, let's do more business." They may candidly admit that they dropped the ball. They may even apologize. But you're done.

I worked with one company that sells an IT cloud solution for recruitment and hiring. It's a powerful and useful product—if people actually use it.

In most cases, things start out great. The salesperson helps the client set up the platform and create some recruiting campaigns.

Over the next three to six months, one of two things happens: either the client is doing a really good job, or never gets around to using it. The contract is for twelve months, and if a client isn't actively using the program by then, you can be sure they won't be renewing the program.

I listened to some client calls. All of them were some variation of the "it's-not-you-it's-me" speech that every brokenhearted teenager has heard: "Oh, we've been really busy." "We lost a couple of key employees." "Well, we're having a lot of success with our other programs and we're concerned using your platform may now be a distraction." "Oh, my job changed; I don't know who's in charge of that now." "I tried it a while ago and couldn't figure it out; I meant to call you, but . . . ".

Are the excuses valid? Maybe. But don't they sound a lot like all those reasons you didn't go to your Weight Watchers meeting?

If you want that renewal, or the next order, or simply a satisfied customer, you have to be willing to make the buyer a bit uncomfortable. You need to be polite and positive, of course. But you need to hold them accountable.

Yet I was seeing that some salespeople in this organization shied away from frank talk. They wanted the client to feel good. They didn't want to "pressure" the client. So they did nothing and hoped things would get better. Or, sometimes, they tried to do the buyer's job for them—for example, by setting up campaigns in the program that the client would never use. We all know how that story ends.

The successful salespeople, on the other hand, were picking up on these issues early and addressing them while they were still manageable. Think again of the Weight Watchers example. If you've only missed a week or two, it's relatively easy to get back on track. But if you haven't been to a meeting in three months, you're probably gone for good. Psychologically, you've moved on.

So the successful salespeople were intervening early—nudging, reminding, coaching, and holding the client accountable to get moving. Did these clients feel pressured? A little, perhaps. But did they resent the salesperson? Not at all. They *wanted* to be pressured, because they wanted the program to succeed. Otherwise, they know they'll find themselves a year later having to explain to someone at their company why they paid all that money for something that didn't work.

So in this case, the most successful salespeople were the ones who set clear goals and expectations from Day One. Typically, the conversations would go something like this:

Salesperson: So let's set a target. How many new customer-service reps will you need to hire this year?

Client: Given our growth targets and attrition rates, we'll need about two hundred.

Salesperson: So to get two hundred good hires, you'll need about one thousand candidates—or a target of eighty-three a month. Does that sound right?

Client: Yes.

Salesperson: Okay, then we need to get started right away. Let me help you set up your first campaign. And let me give you a checklist of things you'll need to do over the next four weeks....

A month later, to the day, the salesperson is calling that client to see how they're doing against that short-term goal. Are they on track, ahead of goal, or behind? If they're behind, why? What does the client need to do to close the gap? What's working and what isn't? For example:

Salesperson: Okay, Kate, I can see that you've only generated fifty applications this month. That's lower than we'd like to see, so let's review what happened and see if we can get it back on track. Let's go through the checklist. Were you able to connect your system with all of the recruiting sites?

Client: Well, no. I connected with two, but I had problems connecting with the other two.

Salesperson: Okay, I'll help you get that done today. Let's move on to Item Two. ...

As they work through the checklist, the salesperson reminds Kate that he's asking these questions because he wants to see her achieve her recruitment goals. He reminds her of what Kate told him at the outset: that hitting those goals is critical to the company's expansion strategy.

And he ends by getting specific commitments: "Excellent, so you'll get that new campaign started by next Wednesday? That's terrific. Let's schedule a call on Friday to review the initial results. How's that sound? Terrific! I'm excited to see you moving forward."

Customer accountability is a must with the sales training I do. As we wrap up each day's session, I ask everyone to stand and think of the one thing that was most valuable and how they will commit to putting it in practice. It's a powerful exercise for managers to observe the takeaway from the sessions and to hear everyone's commitment.

But let's face it: Without follow-up, progress reports, and some attaboy coaching to keep everyone motivated, those commitments will soon be forgotten. That's why we have thirty-day-after conference calls where everyone has to report about a client they called on, the concept from the training they put into practice, the outcome of the call, and what we can learn from this person's actions.

It takes about sixty seconds per person, but it's one of the most valuable things we do. Ninety-four percent of participants have great success stories. Why? Because the follow-up meetings create accountability and follow-through. People know they have to report a success story in thirty days, so they are actively practicing the concept we taught.

It's exhilarating to witness these great results. But frankly, it's also disappointing because sales management should be holding the team accountable. There are times when I have to have some very frank talks with managers. I don't hesitate to say, "You need to step it up, get away from your desk and out with your team. You need to listen to their sales calls, ride along on their customer visits, monitor what they're doing, coach and reinforce these behaviors."

Guess what happens? Nearly always, the sales managers agree. And as a result, they get the outcomes they wanted—and paid for. Everybody wins.

Questions to ask

Here are questions you can use to set and manage expectations at the beginning:

- Let's make sure the goals you've set are exactly what you're looking to achieve and by when.
- Take me through the action steps between now and _____ to ensure you are on target with your goals.
- Challenges are going to get in the way; that's a fact of life. Let's discuss what might be some issues that could surface and how you plan to manage them and not get distracted if they do.
- At the same time, there should be some good opportunities to take advantage of that could help you accelerate your progress toward your goals. Let's talk about what those opportunities could be and how you can focus your time and effort to make them happen.

Here are some ongoing questions to ask as you work through a project or implementation:

- Let's review your progress to date. Let's go back to what we originally agreed to. Where you are you now in relation to your goals? What's working well for you? What's not? Let's not get discouraged; let's first focus on what you've been able to do so far.
- Where do you see hurdles? What are some things you've tried so far to address these hurdles?
- What do you have in mind moving forward? Where can I assist you to keep things moving in the right direction?
- Let's focus on [a short-term objective] between now and _____ . If I commit to do _____ , then you'll commit to do _____ . How's that sound?
- I'm excited to see us getting some new energy going to ensure you achieve the results you're looking for. Now do me a favor: If anything should surface that I need to know about before our next scheduled conversation, you'll let me know? Terrific.

As a salesperson, you can't just expect to close a sale and wash your hands. When you stay engaged and create shared accountabilities, your clients are more likely to achieve the results they were originally looking for. And they'll give you a large share of the credit for their success. They'll happily give you referrals and testimonials—and put you at the top of their preferred-vendor list.

19

Cold Calling Questions
That Get Prospects Talking

COLD CALLING SEEMS to be out of fashion these days.

I'm constantly hearing from companies promoting all kinds of "lead generation" solutions. Of course, there's no question that companies need to generate sales leads. But it seems to me that many of these offerings seem to be promising that advanced marketing technology can finally eliminate the cold sales call—that companies can "nurture" prospects through a process, untouched by human hands, until they are "warm" enough to merit a call from a salesperson.

I'm all for making life easier for salespeople. And it's true that salespeople can no longer afford to engage in the slow, laborious pick-and-shovel prospecting of days gone by. But the idea that salespeople will only be talking to warmed-up, ready-to-buy prospects who are waiting for their call is, frankly, a pipe dream.

Lead-generation programs can help you improve the quality of your prospecting lists, but they don't eliminate cold calls. The reality is that salespeople still need to master the art of reaching out to strangers, quickly overcoming skepticism, and creating a dialogue that can help both parties explore whether there's some basis for doing business.

If cold calling is falling out of fashion, that's good news for salespeople who know how to do it. While other salespeople are waiting for prospects to be gently nurtured, massaged, and guided through a marketing process, you can be speaking to those very same prospects right now.

But let's be honest: Cold calling remains the toughest task in sales.

Conventional wisdom suggests that salespeople are reluctant to cold-call out of fear of rejection. Rejection can be tough to hear, and salespeople hear a lot of it. You will talk to many people who aren't willing or able to buy what you sell.

But a greater source of cold calling anxiety, I believe, is that you're flying blind. Even if you've done your homework on the company, you're speaking with someone about whom you know little or nothing. So how can you sell to them? You don't know her personality, her likes or dislikes, what kind of day she's having, or anything else. You don't know what will resonate with her or what will turn her off.

Your prospects, by the way, face a similar challenge. They don't know a thing about you—which means that they have absolutely no idea whether a conversation with you will be extremely valuable or a complete waste of time.

At that critical juncture, all you're really looking for is *permission to continue the conversation*. And the best way to do that is with well-crafted questions. As I've said earlier, we're highly socialized to answer questions—even when they're posed by a stranger. As long as they're asked respectfully and with worthy intent, we find questions almost impossible to ignore.

Here's a very simple question-based approach to cold calling that can work in virtually any industry and with virtually any prospect:

Establish context. In earlier chapters, I've discussed the need for a brief "elevator pitch"—a quick summation of your value proposition. In a cold call, that speech needs to be stripped down to its barest essentials. Initially, prospects simply can't focus on a complex value proposition, detailed descriptions of what you sell, or how you differ from the competition. They need just enough context to keep listening.

Specifically, they want to know (1) who you are, (2) who you represent, and (3) why you're calling.

For example:

"Hi, Jan. This is Sarah Smith from Remote Surgical Systems. We build software and hardware that allows surgeons to perform operations remotely—even if they're thousands of miles from the operating room. We've worked with several major health systems, including _____ and _____ in your area. The reason I'm calling is because [you recently attended one of our Webinars/ you've just announced plans to expand overseas/we've worked with one of your surgeons in the past/etc.] and I thought we might be able to help you ____."

Ask permission. Next, ask the prospect for permission to ask a few questions:

"Based on our experience with other large health systems like yours, may I ask you a few questions?"

Ask value-building questions. Prospects might be willing to answer one or two of your questions out of politeness. But you need to move quickly to questions that build value, or they'll suddenly find some urgent piece of business that they must attend to.

At the same time, you can't go too deep too fast. Mentally, the prospect is still shifting gears from whatever it was he or she was doing when you called (and possibly hoping to get back to). So after you get their attention, start with simple or straightforward questions that are easy to answer. The goal is to get the prospect focused on the issue you want to discuss.

A first question might be simply, "I understand you're responsible for evaluating new equipment for the surgical suite, is that correct?"

This sounds like a standard qualifying question, but it creates value for the prospect: The reason you're asking is to be sure you're engaging the right person and not wasting anyone's time.

It's at this point, by the way, that many salespeople jump the gun. Having established that Jan is indeed the person who evaluates surgical equipment, they stop asking questions and start telling Jan all about what they have to offer. But that creates no value for Jan. Instead of listening to a salesperson drone on and on, she can just request some literature or a web address where she can get this information at her leisure.

So this is the point where you need to have a powerful question—prepared in advance—that simultaneously achieves two objectives: (1) it signals to the prospect that this call will potentially be worthy of their time, and (2) it gets the prospect talking instead of you.

For example:

"Jan, let me ask: Have you ever looked into remote surgery suites as a way to increase surgery admissions, enhance patient outcomes, and improve market exposure?"

Or:

"Jan, are you familiar with what University Health Systems is doing with remote surgical suites?"

Or:

"Jan, often health systems turn to us because admissions in their smaller hospitals are too low. Is that an issue you're facing?"

Each of these questions promises at least the possibility of value. If Jan believes that you just might strengthen her market position, or give her the inside scoop on what another health system is doing, or help her solve that nagging problem with her small hospital, she'll continue the conversation.

Be ready with follow-up questions. If you can get Jan to answer that first question, it creates an opportunity to follow up with the kinds of questions I've described in the first half of this book. For example, you might use a lock-on question:

Jan: Yes, we have looked at what University Health Systems is doing in this area. It's intriguing, but it seems risky.

You: You said it was intriguing. What specifically was intriguing you and your team?

The objective at this point isn't to sell Jan or refute her objection. It's too early. The goal is to get her talking. She gave you two important clues, the words *intriguing* and *we*. "Intriguing" tells you something sparked her interest and possibly a motive. She also said "we," which tells you other people are involved. That's why you asked about her and her team. The more she tells you about her situation, the more opportunities you have to create value.

So how long should this conversation last? It depends. Some prospects want to get to the point quickly, so you should go for the appointment right away. For others, you've identified something near and dear to their hearts, and/or they have time, so they'll want to talk. Why rush them? Ask good questions. Judge how receptive they are.

But however long the conversation lasts, the key is to move it forward to the next step. You only get so much time before the prospect starts to get impatient or has other things to take care of.

Ask for a next step. Assuming you've determined that the prospect is potentially a good fit, use the preliminary information you've gathered to propose a next step. For example, you don't want to cite chapter and verse about what her competitor is doing or how they addressed the risks. Use that interest to get a meeting. You might say:

It's interesting that you mentioned patient safety. That was the first issue that University Health raised. I have some specific information on how they resolved that question. And you might be interested to learn how they increased surgical admissions by 14 percent in one year, and increased bottom-line revenue by 5 percent as a result of this program. Can we meet next Wednesday at ten so I can show you as well as learn more about your needs?

Here are some more general examples of how to ask for the appointment:

"Well _____ , based on what you've told me, it sounds like we might be able to help you with _____ . When can we schedule a time to meet? (For a long sales cycle.)

"Well, based on what you've told me so far, I think our _____ solution might be worth looking at. May I tell you a little bit about it? (For a short sales cycle.)

Of course, you don't have to follow these five steps in lockstep fashion. You can be flexible, depending on the flow of the call. For example, if I feel I have a receptive prospect or one who is short on time, I'll quickly explain who I am and what we do, and then try to set an appointment. Once I have the meeting scheduled, I'll say something like this: "So that I can prepare for our meeting and you get the most from it, let me ask you a few questions." Then I'll go through a version of the process I've described above.

For the right prospects, this cut-to-the-chase approach works great! It demonstrates respect and that I won't waste their time. The follow-up questions show that I want to be prepared for the scheduled meeting and address what's important to them. The pressure is off, and often they'll keep talking for another five to ten minutes or more.

As part of this preparatory questioning, be sure to ask, "Who else should be involved that would like to learn more about this?" Because you've built rapport and demonstrated respect, prospects will often open up and tell you who else should be involved. Many times they'll reach out to include them in the meeting. Which means you've now got more buy in and a shorter sales cycle.

Will this five-step method turn every prospecting call into a sale? Of course not. Will you still get a lot of nos? Absolutely. But it should make cold calling less stressful and more efficient. It will help you quickly yet respectfully disqualify nonbuyers (and allow you to ask who you should be talking to in their organization). It will position you as a knowledge-able salesperson who might be able to provide value. And perhaps most important, it will give you greater confidence on the call. Instead of flying blind, you have a clear path to follow.

20

Shots in the Dark

IT'S TOUGH TO craft good questions to leave as messages on people's voice mail and email, but it is not impossible. In other sales situations, questions are used to spark a dialogue: You ask a question. The buyer's response leads to another question, and so on.

In voice mail and email, there is no dialogue—at least not in real time. It's all one-sided. You're sending a message into the dark and hoping it will create a spark of interest.

So the purpose of the question is much different. Especially with voice mail, you're unlikely to get a response. Your goal is to prompt the buyer to take your follow-up call or open your next email—and ultimately, to agree to engage in a discussion.

One of the best ways to achieve that is with the educational question (see Chapter 3). Recall that the purpose of an educational question isn't to *gather* information but to *provide* information.

And not any old information. Too many voice mails and emails end up as a product dump, where the salesperson throws a bunch of spaghetti against the wall and hopes something will stick. A true educational question provides some fact, insight, or perspective that prompts buyers to stop and think. It may challenge an assumption they hold, or shine a light on an issue they've overlooked, or suggest a new direction that they hadn't considered. You want your prospect to think, "That's interesting. I'd like to know more, so I'm open to talking to this salesperson."

Voice Mail Examples

Here are some examples of how to use educational questions in a voice mail:

"Kelly, this is Kevin Jones from _____ . According to *JAMA*, there is a case of pneumonia among ventilator patients every week at busy ICUs, and up to 40 percent of these patients die. Over the last twelve months I have been working with a hospital in northern New Jersey, and during that time not one patient on a ventilator has developed pneumonia. Is this something that could be of interest for you? If so, please call me at _____ ." (By the way, even though few prospects will actually call you back, you should always leave a number. For one thing, you might have stumbled across a prospect with an urgent need for what you sell. For another, it signals that *you* believe that the information you'd like to share is worth a return call.)

"Hi, Dan. My name is Amy and I work for _____ . I came across an article in *American Cattleman* that says the average rancher is pushing seventy and looking for better ways to manage their cattle operations—something that's safer and less labor intensive. Is it fair to say you probably have quite a few customers who fit this profile? If so, I have an idea that might help you better serve this market. Please give me a call at _____ ."

"Hi, Lauren. This is Ryan Smith from _____ . Last week I saw a report on CNBC that claimed drug testing is an ineffective tool to weed out poor-quality job applicants. Yet, five times as many companies test for drugs today compared to ten years ago. I've worked with a company in your industry to put in place a better way to screen applicants. They've documented savings of more than $5 million and increased retention rates. Is this something that might be of interest to you? If so, you can reach me at _____ ."

"Hello, Dr. Wilson. The *New England Journal of Medicine* reports that sepsis is one of the top ten causes of hospital morbidity, and kills an average of 42 percent of the people it afflicts. We are working with a number of clinicians who have cut that number in half. Could sepsis be a potential risk in your hospital? Please call me at _____ ."

"Hi, _____ . My name is _____ . *U.S. News & World Report* just reported that over 75 percent of high-tech firms turn to foreign workers to manage their help-desk operations. One of the key challenges seems to be surmounting the language barrier and the difficulty customers have communicating with the help-desk personnel. My company is currently working with a client who has addressed this concern and increased customer retention by 30 percent over the past twelve months. Is this an issue you are experiencing? If so, please call me."

Voice Mail Templates

Here are some templates to help you create educational questions to suit your situation. Simply fill in the blanks.

"Hi, my name is _____ with _____ . I recently came across some information that would be of interest to you. While reading [trade journal X], I learned that _____ . How has your company been affected by this issue? We have some answers. Please call me at _____ ."

"Hi, my name is _____ with _____ . I've learned about some pending legislation that might affect your company. The legislation is _____ . Does your company have a plan in place to deal with this change? Over _____ in your industry have turned to us for solutions."

"Hi, my name is _____ with _____ and I read an article this morning in _____ that claimed _____ . My clients' experiences have been different, however, and I was wondering how your company's experience compares."

Using Email

For email, of course, you can omit your name, company, and phone number, since they're included in your signature. As a result, you can get right to the point.

Here are some examples of how to provoke a customer response via email:

> I am writing to you because my company has had great success working with pharmaceutical companies on new product introductions. We have been able to increase profit margins as much as 32% and reduce time-to-market by 25% Here's the text of a letter of thanks that my company received from [a leader in the field that will inspire trust in the prospective customer] detailing the success it has had thanks to our system. I will call this Friday morning to introduce myself. How is 8:30 a.m. CST?

> I happened to be reading an article in the *Wall Street Journal* that I thought would be of interest to you. The article quoted an industry insider saying that firms specializing in property and casualty insurance should expect record growth in the next five years. Tom, I was just wondering if you had seen the article and what you thought about it.

> We are currently working with a number of firms that are already experiencing double-digit growth. If you have a chance, either drop me a line or give me a call at _____ and I can share some ideas I have with you. Otherwise I will call you early next week to introduce myself. Thanks!

> Just this morning I read an article in the *Washington Post* that said that employees in large companies spend an average of two hours each day on the Internet for personal reasons. I'm curious to learn if you are looking to address this issue. My company's product has helped other large corporations cut this time in half. If you think this is something you'd like to learn more about, please contact me. Or I can call you Friday morning if that works better for you.

> In a recent LinkedIn Survey, 19% of respondents said health insurance was the primary driving factor in taking, leaving, or keeping a job. I am contacting you to share some ideas on how you can select and customize the most cost effective plan that will continue to attract

and retain your top talent. What's your availability Monday after 11:00 a.m. for me to give you a call?

I am writing to you because I came across an article (see attached document) on _____ website. The article cited a study comparing the sales practices of various building-products manufacturers, and found that working through real-estate agents is proving to be especially effective.

We are currently working with several building-products manufacturers who are trying this approach. As a result of our efforts, our clients are reporting on average a 15 percent increase in sales. I'd like to discuss their results with you. I'll be visiting a client in your area next Thursday. How about I stop by your office around 10:00 a.m.?

Email Templates

Here are some templates to use in constructing your educational questions for email.

I am writing to you because I recently read an article in _____ that I thought would be of interest to you. The article claimed _____.
Is this something you are concerned about? If so, we have some answers for you.

I have attached an article I thought would be informative for you. The article states, "_____." I think that this [trend/legislation/demographic] provides an opportunity for your business. Are you interested in learning about some ideas that would take advantage of this opportunity? If so, you can reach me at _____.

CAN-SPAM and Email

The federal CAN-SPAM Act imposes certain requirements that you need to observe for prospecting emails. Many people assume that these requirements only apply to bulk email campaigns, but in fact they apply to any commercial email. CAN-SPAM excludes what are known as "transactional or relationship" emails—for example, an email advising a current customer that their order has shipped—but if the primary intent of the email is to promote or sell something, the rules apply. Fortunately, those rules are fairly simple, and they won't prevent you from sending the kinds of respectful, thoughtful emails we've described in this chapter.

Here are the main requirements, according to the Federal Trade Commission. If you're not sure your emails are in compliance, check with your marketing department:

1. **Don't use false or misleading header information.** Your "From," "To," "Reply-To," and routing information—including the originating domain name and email address—must be accurate and identify the person or business who initiated the message.

2. **Don't use deceptive subject lines.** The subject line must accurately reflect the content of the message.

3. **Identify the message as an ad.** The law gives you a lot of leeway in how to do this, but you must disclose clearly and conspicuously that your message is an advertisement.

4. **Tell recipients where you're located.** Your message must include your valid physical postal address. This can be your current street address, a post office box you've registered with the U.S. Postal Service, or a private mailbox you've registered with a commercial mail receiving agency established under Postal Service regulations.

5. **Tell recipients how to opt out of receiving future email from you.** Your message must include a clear and conspicuous explanation of how the recipient can opt out of getting email from you in the future. Craft the notice in a way that's easy for an ordinary person to recognize, read, and understand. Creative use of type size, color, and location can improve clarity. Give a return email address or another easy Internet-based way to allow people to communicate their choice to you. You may create a menu to allow a recipient to opt out of certain types of messages, but you must include the option to stop all commercial messages from you. Make sure your spam filter doesn't block these opt-out requests.

6. **Honor opt-out requests promptly.** Any opt-out mechanism you offer must be able to process opt-out requests for at least thirty days after you send your message. You must honor a recipient's opt-out request within ten business days. You can't charge a fee,

require the recipient to give you any personally identifying information beyond an email address, or make the recipient take any step other than sending a reply email or visiting a single page on an Internet website as a condition for honoring an opt-out request. Once people have told you they don't want to receive more messages from you, you can't sell or transfer their email addresses, even in the form of a mailing list. The only exception is that you may transfer the addresses to a company you've hired to help you comply with the CAN-SPAM Act.

7.   **Monitor what others are doing on your behalf.** The law makes clear that even if you hire another company to handle your email marketing, you can't contract away your legal responsibility to comply with the law. Both the company whose product is promoted in the message and the company that actually sends the message may be held legally responsible.

Some Final Considerations

Here are some additional ways to make voice mail and email more effective:

Don't send generic messages. They won't help you get business and will probably hurt you. Make sure your emails are specific, personable, and have a call to action.

Don't expect a reply. Most prospects won't respond. That's okay. The real value is that you've exposed them to your message, so your follow-up call will have some context. Go ahead and suggest that the prospect call you—it communicates that you believe in the value of what you sell—but let them know that if they don't call you within a specified time frame, that you'll take the initiative and call them.

Be persistent. When prospecting, it takes an average of eight to ten touch points—some type of communication—to connect with a prospect. Most salespeople give up way before that. Be one of the few who sticks to a rigorous follow-up plan.

Change your message when you follow up. The worst voice mails and emails are the "checking in" ones: "I'm following up on my previous message," or "I'm just checking in to make sure you got my last email/ voice mail," or "I thought I'd touch base again." These add no value to the prospect. Instead, offer something new: a new story, a compelling question, a brief success story, a different reason to buy. After all, your previous attempt may have missed the mark. Focus on a new motivation or pain point.

Use postal mail to stand out. Mail an article, handwrite some notes, or use a highlighter or a sticky note to demonstrate this information is specifically for the prospect. You'll make a greater impact, and there's much less chance an assistant will trash it. Then follow up with a phone call and an email.

Engage assistants. If you are calling on C-suite executives—presidents, owners, CEOs or VPs, for example—many will have an executive assistant. Don't view them as obstacles; view them as people who can amplify your message. They sit in on executive meetings, manage their bosses' calendars, and understand the organization—in some cases, better than their bosses. Call on them and ask for their help. Give them the same respect you'd give their bosses.

Think beyond nine to five. Many prospects look at their emails 24/7. You may be more likely to get a response off hours when the contact is catching up on emails, especially during the weekend. If you're calling—especially a high-level decisionmaker—the best time to call is often before 8:00 a.m. or after 5:00 p.m.—when the receptionists are not screening calls and they're not likely to be in meetings. Most automated systems have a directory and give out the extension that you can make note of when you try again.

21

Your Very Best Prospects

Using Referral Questions to Build Your Own Pipeline

DESPITE ALL THE new ideas floating around on how to find prospects—for example, social media, email blasting, Internet databases—referrals are still the most effective strategy. In fact, in a technology-enabled world, they're more important than ever.

Think about it: Technology is supposed to keep us all connected, but it's actually made it harder than ever to reach prospects. They don't answer their phones. They don't return our calls. They don't respond to our emails.

Technology has made outreach ridiculously cheap, but the result is that prospects are bombarded by sales and marketing folks trying to get their attention. Prospects tune these messages out. They're more cynical, cautious, and distrustful than ever. With so many salespeople clamoring for their attention, they keep hearing the same pitch again and again. Even if there is some potential value buried in their inbox, buyers don't have the time or energy to dig it out. Their biggest problem is how to manage the onslaught.

That's why *trust* is the number-one factor in doing business today. When a customer gives you the name of a colleague or friend, they're entrusting you with something very precious: their own business relationships. They need to believe that you won't make a fool of them, and that you won't put those relationships in jeopardy in any way. Of course they must trust you to be professional and courteous. But that's not enough. They also must trust that you will potentially add value to the person they've referred to you.

Why Don't Salespeople Ask for Referrals?

Given the power of referrals, I'm always amazed at how few salespeople ask for them consistently.

Too often salespeople wait for the perfect time to ask for referrals. It's too early in the relationship. Or it's too late. Or we just sent an invoice. Or we're about to send an invoice. Or the account will be in better shape next month.

Whether your focus is on managing accounts or prospecting, every salesperson should always be looking for new business. And that means *always* asking for referrals.

The real problem isn't timing. It's fear.

Salespeople are afraid that if they ask, the customer will say something like this: "No, I can't think of anyone right now." Or, "It's a little early. Let's wait and see how this project turns out." Or, "I really don't give out my contacts." Or they're afraid of what the customer *isn't* saying, but might be thinking: "What if you harass or annoy my contacts and they come back and ask me why I gave them your name?" Or, "Are you kidding me? I would never recommend you." Or, "If I give you other contacts and you get their business, then I'll get less attention."

These anxieties really come down to fear of rejection. It's hard enough to be rejected by a prospect. It's far worse to think about rejection from an established customer. So your mind tends to catastrophize. You wonder if you've earned the right to ask for a referral. Or if you are doing a good enough job. Or if you'll be seen as trying to exploit your current relationship. Or if the relationship isn't as solid as you think.

Ultimately, we hesitate to ask for referral when we *don't believe that we're creating enough value.*

Imagine that your job is to go around handing out hundred-dollar bills. You've just given one to your customer. Would you feel awkward asking, "Do you know anyone else who could use a hundred bucks?" Would your customer hesitate to give you names? Of course not.

Well, isn't that what you're doing when you ask for a referral? Presumably, you've created a lot more than a hundred dollars' worth of value for your customer. So if you believe in your own value proposition, why wouldn't you ask for a referral? And why wouldn't your contact give you one?

Some salespeople have the opposite problem. They think they've delivered so much value that they shouldn't *have* to ask for a referral. "If I'm doing a good job, my work will speak for itself," they tell themselves. "My customer will sing my praises and all I have to do is wait for the phone to ring." But even when customers love you, that usually doesn't happen. Nor should it. It's not our customers' job to drum up new business for us. *We* have to take the initiative and ask for referrals.

How to Ask for a Referral

Assuming you've established that you can deliver value, the ask goes something like this:

"Who are two or three individuals that you admire and respect in your [company, department, division, engineering society, association, buyers co-op, church community, etc.] who might want to benefit from [increasing their sales, reducing costs, saving time, eliminating risks, gaining a competitive edge, or whatever benefit you deliver to your customers]?"

It sounds simple enough. But there are two key elements to keep in mind:

1. **Narrow it down.** Ask about specific groups or individuals within their network, and only ask for a few names at most. If you ask, "Is there anybody you can think of who can use our services?" your contacts have to work *way* too hard. They have to flip through their mental contact list looking for a fit. Most likely you'll get, "I can't think of anyone," or "I'll get back to you."

   Instead, imagine a question like this: "XYZ Industries has been on my prospect list for a long time. I know you worked there at one time. Is there anyone there who might be willing to direct me to the right person to talk to?" This focused approach makes it easier for your customer to help you. She only needs to focus on XYZ Industries.

   Another benefit of a narrow focus is that it allows you to ask for referrals more than once. If you ask the "is there anyone you know" question over and over, your buyer will eventually get impatient. But not if you're asking about XYZ Industries this month, the Chamber of Commerce next month, and ABC Corp the month after that.

2.   **Don't just ask about potential buyers.** You'll notice that I said "individuals that you admire or respect." If you limit yourself to "buyers," you increase the odds that your contact will draw a blank. Similarly, in the XYZ example, your customer doesn't need to think of someone who might buy from you. Any contact will do. You can take it from there.

When your customer gives you one or more names, use the questioning techniques we've discussed in earlier chapters to learn more. For example: "So what is it about Allison that you admire and respect?" Or, "Can you tell me something about Joe that I should know before I talk to him?" You get valuable insight into your customer's relationship with this person. And you have a great icebreaker when you connect with Allison or Joe.

Who to Ask

There's no reason to limit yourself to customers when you ask for a referral. You can also ask:

Prospects who said no. Obviously, you can't expect to get a referral from a prospect who's blown you off. But if you've established some dialogue, only to learn that the timing isn't right, or the budget isn't there, or the fit isn't good, the prospect may be willing to point you in a better direction. And there's no harm in asking. You might say something like this: "I appreciate you being forthright with me and I'm sorry we can't assist you at this time. So let me ask you—who are two or three individuals that you admire and respect who might benefit from . . . ?"

Noncompeting companies. If you meet people in a related but noncompeting company—especially salespeople—they can be a rich source of referrals. For example, if you're at an industry networking event, don't limit yourself to looking for potential customers. Look for people who serve the same customers as you, but sell something different. Be prepared to give as well as get; if you want them to share their contacts, you'll have to share yours. Otherwise the same rules apply: Be specific to make it easier for the other person to help you. For example: "Have you had any luck calling on Company _____ ? Can you give me a name? I can't get past the receptionist."

Family, friends, etc. Some salespeople are reluctant to mix business with family or friends. That's understandable. But referrals are something different. You're not asking your personal contacts to buy from you or even recommend you. You're simply asking them to help you identify potential leads. These connections can be especially powerful because they're outside of your business network, so they're less likely to lead you to the "usual suspects."

Former customers and less-than-satisfied customers. Don't rule out former customers, or even current customers where things haven't always gone smoothly. As with prospects who've said no, they may recognize that what you sell may be a better fit for someone else.

Mavens, gurus, and influencers. Sometimes your best referral source isn't a customer or prospect, but someone who *influences* customers and prospects. For example, if there's a professor who's a recognized expert in your field, or a consultant who's worked with the top companies in your industry, that's a relationship you want to cultivate. Winning referrals from these sources is a long-term project because their reputation is their stock in trade. So they will be *very* judicious in whom they're willing to refer. The key is showing that you really *can* create unique value for their constituencies—that you will be an asset to their reputation, not a liability. Often, the best way to approach them is to ask for their advice and counsel. To find them, ask existing customers: "Whose opinion do *you* respect?"

Whether working with existing customers or other referral sources, be sure to reassure them if you sense any hesitation about giving you names. You might say, "I'll simply see if I can help them out. If they're all taken care of, I'll be on my way." And, of course, be sure to honor that promise. Word will get back.

Approaching the Referral

Ideally, your referral source will make an introduction for you. But you can't always count on it. If you're going in cold, your opening statement might go something like this:

Salesperson: Hi, Allison. My name is _____ and I work for _____. Tom Higgins suggested I reach out to you. I've been working with Tom to help get his company's products into international markets, and he thought you might see some benefit in a similar program.

Prospect: Oh, you work with Tom? How is he?

Salesperson: He's great. He's a big fan of yours. In fact, he told me—and I quote—"Allison is always looking for ways to stay a step ahead of the competition."

With this brief exchange, you've sidestepped all those barriers that I mentioned at the beginning of this chapter. You've already begun to establish a connection with Allison. She'll probably at least give you a fair hearing. And not coincidentally, you've enhanced Tom's relationship with Allison by passing along what he told you.

22

Social Selling

Adapting Tried-and-True Questions for a New Medium

SALESPEOPLE NEED TO be savvy users of social media. More and more, it's where your buyers will be living. At the same time, it's no panacea. Leads aren't going to suddenly start rolling in. And it can seem so daunting that many salespeople avoid it. They'll put together a LinkedIn page, connect with colleagues and perhaps some customers, and call it a day.

I get it. If you tried to do everything that social-selling evangelists recommend, you could spend all day every day working your social media accounts with not much to show for it. Salespeople need to spend most of their time doing what only they can do—personally interacting with living, breathing buyers. So the challenge for working salespeople is how to use social media strategically. They need to invest their most precious resource—their time—where it will yield the most results.

Social media is especially useful in two areas: (1) getting referrals to qualified prospects, and (2) positioning yourself to prospects and existing buyers as a thought leader—an expert in your field who can provide valuable insights. As we'll see, the questioning techniques you've learned in this book can help you do both.

Asking for Referrals

The referral techniques in Chapter 21 apply to social media as well. But social media platforms such as LinkedIn create some unique challenges. (By the way, I'm focusing on LinkedIn in this discussion because it's specifically built for business networking. You may get a lot more pushback on other platforms.)

Let's start with building your network. You probably have a lot of contacts already. After all, it's your job to talk to people whose business interests intersect with your own. It's simple to invite buyers and prospects into your network. And you should.

However, keep in mind that in the world of social media, you are judged by the *quality* of your network. So be judicious about whom you invite and whom you accept invitations from. Paradoxically, more names may create less value. If you have ten thousand contacts in your network, it may look like you're just harvesting names. So the people who really matter to you may be reluctant to accept your invitation. They may be worried about being exposed to scammers and spammers.

It's hard to have a hard-and-fast guide in terms of how many contacts you should have. But here's a rule of thumb: You should know nearly everyone in your network well enough that you'd be comfortable emailing them or calling them, and they'd be comfortable enough with you to respond.

Here's an often-overlooked reality: The real power for networking through social media is less about *your* network and more about the networks of your *contacts*. When you connect to someone on LinkedIn, they get to see your network. And you get to see theirs.

Those networks represent a valuable pool of potential business for you, because *they resemble your contacts*. Many will be in the same industry. Many will have similar jobs, similar experience, or similar responsibilities.

Getting referrals via LinkedIn involves two questions: (1) Will you connect with me? And (2) Will you connect me with ___?

Will you connect with me?

Some asks are easy: friends, colleagues, customers, people you've worked with in the past. But they only get you so far. The people you know tend to know the people you know. For the purpose of referrals, the most valuable contacts are the ones you *don't* know as well.

You'll get more connections from this group if your request creates value, or potential value, for the person you're reaching out to.

For example, let's say you just got off the phone with Chris. You had a pleasant conversation, but she's not currently in a position to buy from you.

Instead of using the generic "I'd like to connect with you" template, you might use a message like this:

> Hi, Chris. Great talking to you today. Thanks for helping me under-
> stand what your company does in greater detail. I can think of two
> contacts who might be interested in the services your company offers,
> and I'd be happy to make an introduction. May I add you to my pro-
> fessional network?

Or:

> Hi, Chris. Great talking to you today. After we spoke, it occurred
> to me that my former colleague Joe Smith recently faced a challenge
> similar to the one you're facing. If you'd like to get his perspective, I'd
> be happy to connect the two of you. May I add you to my professional
> network?

Or:

> Hi, Chris. Great talking to you today. You mentioned that your
> company is looking to hire a new IT director. I can think of a couple
> of people in my network who might be good candidates, and I'd be
> happy to share their profiles with you if you're interested. May I add
> you to my professional network?

Or let's say you stumble across a name on LinkedIn that you'd like to connect with. You don't know them and they don't know you. You don't have anyone to make an introduction. Asking to connect with someone out of the blue could come across as creepy—unless you provide a plausible reason for your request. If someone has com-mented on your post. If you've commented on theirs. If you belong to the same online group. If you both worked at the same place in the past, even if you didn't know each other. If something on their profile suggests that you have a shared experience or related background. Ide-ally, the reason should be related to what you sell, but it can't be "to sell you something." You must earn that right.

Will you connect me with _____?

The second step in your referral strategy, asking for an introduction, must also create value.

Social media etiquette suggests that it's best to put some time between these two requests. It's also the right way to think about your contacts. You don't want them to feel that you're just using them as a stepping-stone to get to a "real" buyer.

In social media as in everything else, the relationship comes first. Think of your contacts as *assets* that can grow and yield multiple dividends over time. You don't want to cash them in right away. You might reach out to them later to help you gain some insight into the market. Or if you're pursuing an active lead six months from now, their name might come up as a mutual contact. So you might want to wait a while before you start mining a contact's network for referrals. At that point, asking for the referral seems more like a natural extension of the relationship.

So, for example, six months after you connected with Chris, you might reach out to her again:

Hey, Chris. I noticed that you're connected to Gene at XYZ Company. XYZ has been on my list for some time, but I haven't had much luck connecting with them. Do you think Gene could point me in the right direction?

Part of the implicit value in this request, of course, is that Chris knows you will respond in kind if she ever needs an introduction. But research suggests that there's more than a potential quid pro quo at stake. People attach *social* value to a request for help. Responding to a sincere request for help makes people feel better about themselves— *even if they get nothing in return.*

Think about the implications of that. Many salespeople fear that asking for a referral is an imposition. But the ask itself creates value.

Note the word *sincere,* however. People don't feel good about doing a favor if they feel they're being taken advantage of. So limit your ask. Do your homework and find one or two high-value contacts you'd like to connect with. Then show the buyer how much this favor means to you: You let Chris know that XYZ is an important prospect for you. You told her that you've had no luck so far. She can see that helping you out could be a big favor indeed, yet one that would cost her little.

Of course, some people are uncomfortable making introductions no matter what, and of course you need to respect that. But others are reluctant because they fear you will diminish the value of *their* relationship with the contact. Nobody wants to sic a pushy, unprepared salesperson on a friend or colleague.

- The way you ask for the referral can help put such fears to rest. Communicate exactly why you want the introduction and what you will do with it—for example, you need someone to "point you in the right direction" or you'd like to "see if there's a fit with what we do." Soft, tentative language like this will reassure *your* contact that you won't take advantage of the favor. You need to show that you won't embarrass them.

Using Social Media to Increase Your Visibility and Credibility

The other way social media can help you sell is by elevating your visibility and positioning yourself as a thought leader in the industries you serve.

It seems like a slam dunk. You sign up for the biggest LinkedIn interest groups in the industry you serve. You avoid overt selling. You upload posts full of useful knowledge. You repost content that you like. You start conversations. Pretty soon the world is beating a path to your door.

Not likely. For one thing, everybody else is doing the same thing. And it's hardly a level playing field. Some companies have whole departments that do nothing else. They're also paying a lot of money to get preferential positioning for their posts. The little guy hardly stands a chance.

Also, you may find that the audience isn't all it's cracked up to be. Many of the people in those groups will be other salespeople, not potential prospects for you. And out of all those thousands of people who signed up for the group, relatively few of them actively engage on a regular basis. It's usually a handful of the usual suspects who turn up again and again.

So what can you do?

Creating good content takes a lot of time and effort. Asking questions about *other people's* good content takes less time, and can be a good way to boost your visibility. In some ways, a question is more effective than a comment or even a post, because it *invites a response*.

Good questions demonstrate your expertise without being self-promotional. The idea is to become a thought leader not by sharing what you know or think, but by stimulating others to think differently. Do it consistently and people will notice.

Use Educational Questions

Social media is ideal both for *posing* and *creating* educational questions (see Chapter 3).

For example, you can repost an article, blog post, or research study that would interest your buyers, and ask for feedback. It might be as simple as, "Does this ring true to members of this group? Can anyone share their experience?"

You can also pose questions or start conversations that yield highly targeted fodder for your own educational questions. For example:

You sell a self-cleaning glass that can reduce the need to wash windows in skyscrapers. You need to get architects to specify the glass, even though it costs more.

So pose a question in your *facilities management* group, asking members how often their buildings use window washers, how much it costs, how long it takes, and so on. Then turn around and use those responses to create an educational question for *architects*: "I recently asked facilities managers how often they washed their windows, and how much it costs. They told me they typically spend upwards of $200,000 a year on window-washing services. They also said they're extremely concerned about the liability issues of having crews working on scaffolds hundreds of feet in the air. How does that compare with your clients' experience?"

To get the best responses, pose questions that strike an emotional chord. Give people a chance to vent. For example:

- What's the task at work that you most wish you could take off your plate?
- On average, companies spend _____ a year on _____ . Do they get their money's worth? Why or why not?
- Congress is debating a bill to _____ . Some say it will make our industry stronger. Others say it will lead to needless and costly regulation. What do you think?

You don't have to spend a lot of time creating these questions. Sit down and craft twelve good ones. Post one a month. Post them in different forums, in slightly different terms. See which ones get the most passionate responses. That will help you craft even better questions going forward. It may also give you some new insights on how to connect with prospects and customers. Best of all, it puts you in the driver's seat: You're initiating the dialogue and can respond intelligently to the responses.

Follow the Rules

The one thing you *can't* do in these groups is post promotional or sales-focused content. (See the sidebar, which provides LinkedIn's rules for groups.) Don't post product announcements and press releases. You'll quickly find yourself disinvited.

That doesn't mean you can't talk about what you do or about your clients. You can't say, "Eight out of ten of my clients say we've made a significant impact on their bottom line." But it's probably okay to say, "I was speaking to a client the other day, and she raised an issue I hadn't encountered before: _____ . What do you think? Is this something others are seeing, too? What are people doing about it?"

Of course, you can post pretty much whatever you want on your personal page. But here, too, it's probably best to avoid overt selling or highly promotional language. Remember, most of the people who encounter your page won't be actively looking to buy what you sell. But they may be highly valuable contacts nonetheless, so you don't want to drive them away with a sales pitch. And if you do happen to connect with an active buyer, you'll want to bring those conversations offline.

Self-Promotion in Groups

Here's what LinkedIn says about what's acceptable and what's not in group discussions:

While the specific details of what's considered self-promotion depends on the group, topics such as webinars, books, blogs, motivational speaking events, software sales, and real estate can be considered self-promotion. Try to avoid words like "buy," "sell," or "attend."

One way to think of it is to make sure you're talking with people and not talking at them. Here are some tips to posting content and making sure they are in line with the group's goals:

- Check out existing discussions to see what's welcome and what people respond to. Posts that don't get comments are likely not getting the group's attention.
- Post more than just a link. Help people see why your post is relevant and encourage discussion.
- Read the group rules. If the group doesn't have rules, send a note to group management for guidance.

Make the most of your group by using the same etiquette you'd use to interact at a social event or a friend's house.

Here are some best practices to help you become a valued group member:

- Make sure your conversations are relevant to the interests and intent of the group.
- Invite discussion. Ask for members' input on a topic or article that you share and phrase your update as a question.
- If you find yourself disagreeing in a conversation, remember to keep discussion respectful.
- Avoid postings that may be seen as self-promotion.
- If you're sharing a link or article, provide context on its relevance to the group.
- If you're sharing a job opening with a group, post it under the *Jobs* tab.
- This is your group, so you can report spam when you see it. Reporting spam helps everybody in the group, and it helps identify trends so you can prevent similar activity in all groups.

Note: When fellow group members or group management feel that certain contributions don't meet their group's intent, they can take actions like reporting or removing comments, or even removing and blocking you from a group. They monitor the frequency of those actions, and if too many occur, you could become subject to moderation in all your groups for a period of time.

23

The Keys to the Castle:

Questions for Gatekeepers

FOR MOST OF my career in sales, the dreaded Gatekeeper was a figure to be feared. "Real" buyers hid deep within organizations, while receptionists and secretaries kept pesky salespeople at bay.

These days, few companies have the resources to maintain large support staffs, and the few gatekeepers who are left have largely been defanged by automated phone directories, social media, and voice mail.

I sort of wish for the good old days. At least you could engage with a living, breathing human being.

That said, you'll still encounter gatekeepers, especially as you move up the ladder toward higher-value prospects. Front-line people—even those holding important positions—may be expected to answer their own phones (or not, and let calls go to voice mail). But top executives will still rely on personal assistants to help them manage their time and control access. Sometimes these gatekeepers wield considerable power. Sometimes they can be your ally. But at the end of the day, you still need to connect with someone who can actually buy what you sell.

The Initial Encounter

When you speak with a gatekeeper, be brief. Of course, be courteous and respectful, but also speak with authority and confidence. Often I've seen salespeople approach a gatekeeper with a tentative, almost apologetic tone. They ask who's in charge of buying whatever, and would it be possible to speak to them? They act as if they're imposing on the gatekeeper by asking him to do his job!

Almost invariably, the gate slams shut. "I'm not allowed to give out names," the gatekeeper says. "Send an email to the address on our website and if we're interested, someone will get in touch."

The reason salespeople get that reaction is because their tone and demeanor suggests that they're asking for something but have nothing of value to offer in return. That's called begging, and it's beneath you.

If you truly believe that you provide value to your customers, you won't find yourself apologizing or begging. And you will project that confidence to the gatekeeper. Assume that you're going to get through to a decisionmaker because you deserve to. You're not showing up empty-handed. You have something to discuss that the decisionmaker is going to want to know about. Make the gatekeeper conclude that it's safer to say yes than no to you.

Asking for a Name

For example, your opening statement to a gatekeeper might go something like this:

> "Good morning. My name is Bob from the _____ Company. Perhaps you can help me. I'm going to forward some information to the person responsible for _____ . Who would that be?"

Right off the bat, you've disarmed the gatekeeper. You didn't ask to be put through to anyone. They don't have to decide whether you're going to waste the decisionmaker's time. All you need is a name.

You'll probably get it. But if not, stay confident and in control: "I do understand. But it's important that the information doesn't get misplaced or lost. Who should it go to?"

If the gatekeeper still won't give you a name, be gracious and bow out. Obviously you hit a brick wall with the receptionist because it's her job to block unsolicited calls. So shift gears: "Okay. I understand. So let's do this. Please forward me over to the _____ Department, and I'll hold. Thank you."

Here's a secret about even the most recalcitrant gatekeepers: Their goal is to get rid of you. They can be curt, bordering on rude. *But they'll almost never hang up on you.* So don't argue, but don't go away. Gentle persistence is the key. Eventually they'll decide the best way to get rid of you is by forwarding you to someone else.

Once you get past the first line of defense, the going usually gets easier. One of two things will happen: Someone will pick up the phone, or you'll land in someone's voice mail. Either way, you got what you came for: a name.

If someone picks up the phone in the other department, their primary job will almost certainly be something other than screening calls. So you won't get that same reflexive resistance. They're probably in the middle of doing something else and the quickest way to get back to it is to give you what you're asking for. Start by asking for *their* name, if they didn't give it to you. Then use the same approach you used with the primary gatekeeper.

Approaching Gatekeepers When You Have a Name

In this day and age, with Google, social media, and business databases a click away, it's likely that you'll already have a name when you encounter a gatekeeper. Use it to your best advantage. If you say, "Hi, this is Bob Jones. Is Sarah Smith available?" you're giving the gatekeeper the power to say no. Instead, say something like this: "Hi, this is Bob Jones. Please do me a favor and forward me over to Sarah Smith. I'll hold. Thank you."

This approach works very well. You're not asking the gatekeeper for permission; you're asking him to *do* something. And you're communicating the idea that Sarah Smith will want to talk to you. I'm not suggesting that you be deceptive or try to pretend that you know Sarah when you've never met her. But you do have something important to share with Sarah. Your positive attitude about yourself and your products needs to come across in your voice.

Of course, there is a difference between confidence and arrogance. Receptionists and gatekeepers have to deal with all kinds of people all day long. Some will be rude, dismissive, or condescending. Some will try to bully or intimidate them. Don't be one of them. Make their day a little better, not worse. Be positive, courteous, and friendly.

24

C-Suite Questions

How to Connect with Top-Level Executives

FOR MANY SALESPEOPLE, reaching the C-suite is the Holy Grail. If only they can get a few magical moments with the president, owner, CEO, board member, vice president, or director, they've got it made.

It doesn't really work that way. C-level execs delegate operational tasks, which includes buying stuff. Often the person who can say yes is further down on the organizational chart. There's nothing wrong with that. Go where the money is.

But when you have an opportunity to make a bigger impact on an organization—when what you sell aligns with high-level strategy and direction—the C-suite is where you want to be. And when you get that opportunity, you don't want to be telling. You want to be asking.

The key point to remember when you're crafting questions for these prospects is that they're always thinking about the big picture. Like everyone else, they have day-to-day responsibilities. But their *primary* job—the reason they get paid the big bucks—is to set strategy and make sure it gets executed. They are thinking ahead, constantly trying to figure out where they are leading their team.

In the C-suite, you don't hear the kinds of excuses that low-level contacts are likely to give you. You don't hear, "I'm just trying to get through my day. I can't even think beyond what I'm doing now. I'm satisfied with our current situation, no need for change. I can't wait for the weekend."

Getting through the day is a foreign concept to top execs. They're not even thinking about today. They're thinking six months, a year, three, five years out. They embrace change because they know that if they just keep doing what they're doing the world will leave them and their organization

209

behind. They are thinking about growth, competitive advantage, how to position their organizations for future success, and how to respond to emerging threats.

The biggest mistake salespeople make with C-suite executives is to try to sell them the same way they sell to operations people. "Let me tell you about my products and services, my features and benefits," the salesperson says. "Let me tell you about our satisfied customers and why we're better than the competition." Top execs have no patience for that. That's a conversation you should be having with one of their people.

The only reason a C-level executive is willing to give you their time is because they think you might be able to help them with *their* job. They want you to help them think better. They want to be challenged. They want new ideas. They want to know what they've overlooked. Don't let them down.

One of the best ways to initiate this type of high-level discussion is with educational questions, which we discussed in Chapter 3. You will recall that these questions are built around some highly relevant and provocative insight or piece of information that offers a fresh insight about the customer's world or the issues they're facing.

C-suite executives love these questions. They align perfectly with their high-level, strategic thought processes. Top execs love to talk about industry trends, new and innovative ideas, market changes, and challenges.

So prepare for C-level conversations by finding an article, journal, or industry problem that's relevant to the C-suite's industry. Use it as an opener:

"I came across an article that mentioned _____ . It made me think of you. . . . ."

"I do a lot of work in the _____ industry. All of a sudden it seems as if everybody's talking about _____ . Some of my contacts are telling me _____ . Others are saying that's not the case, and it's more about _____ . I'm curious about your thoughts."

"I was at a conference last month, and one of the speakers said _____ . I hadn't really considered that idea before, but it makes a lot of sense. Is it something you're seeing in your business?"

Notice that these examples never mention a particular client or share confidential information. But they do show your keen awareness of the industry and that you, like the exec, are thinking about the big picture.

Tell Me Your Story

If you really want to make a positive, lasting impression on business owners and high-level decisionmakers, ask them about themselves. Successful people love to talk about how they became successful, and few people actually want to hear their story. Their employees and spouses are tired of hearing about it. Their kids just roll their eyes when they start talking about how things were back in the day. Colleagues and peers might be envious and don't want to listen to a rundown of all of their successes. These influential people have a story to tell, and no one who wants to hear it.

How do you get them to share their story with you? During an initial meeting, you can say something like, "You must have had some exciting and challenging times to get this business to where it is today. Can you tell me what prompted you to start your company?" Or, "How did you get started in this business?"

Most likely, this person is going to be thrilled to share her story with you. You can ask follow-up questions during the conversation, but keep the focus on the prospect. This is a golden question and will definitely leave a lasting impression on whomever you ask.

I personally love to hear people's stories because it gives me an insight into their personalities. You also learn that every successful person has struggled and failed, but that they were ultimately able to climb their way back to the top. It is something that we as salespeople can relate to as well. You might even learn something!

By the way, while this technique works great in the C-suite, you can use it elsewhere with great effect. I recently asked this question to a departmental supervisor. It turned out she was a single mom who put herself through college while working nights and raising her children. She is an inspiring person, and it was great to connect with her on a personal level. I am sure she will also remember me, and would be willing to talk to me again and introduce me to others in her organization.

Another way to connect with C-suiters is to ask questions about their organization. It's their baby and they take immense pride in its successes. So you might say, for example:

"I read that your company won an award/was recognized/has achieved/been in business for eighty-eight years and you're the third generation/has a reputation for/has had quite a successful track record in/is known for. . . . Tell me what you believe has led your company (or you) to be where you (or your company) is today? As you look back, what do you believe is the reason why you not only survived but thrived all these years?"

Sit back because you'll get an earful of the company's history, including the challenges, opportunities, people, changes, and how they overcame hurdles. As long as you are genuine and you're truly interested, it's a great question. But if you're just trying to flatter the exec, don't bother. Most top execs recognize brown-nosing when they see it, because they see a lot of it. Don't be a lap dog or cheerleader. Rise to their level.

Don't be afraid to challenge what they tell you. Top execs like to think, articulate, work through problems, identify alternatives. They welcome great questions—even ones that create some discomfort—because they want to stretch their minds.

For the most part, they're friendly and approachable. Their number-one strengths are people and communication skills, which is how they got where they are. They get results through other people, so if you can bring value, they *want* you to engage them.

More C-Suite Questions

Here are some additional C-suite questions:

- What changes are you seeing in the marketplace and how are you and your company dealing with change?
- Where do you see the opportunities moving forward? How are you and your team taking advantage of these opportunities?
- Tell me where you see you and your company three years from now. What are your plans to get there?
- As you reflect back over the past _____ years leading your company, what's the biggest challenge you've had to tackle when it comes

to _____ ? What was the key lesson others can learn from that experience?

- What have you tried that's worked? What have you tried that hasn't worked? What did you learn from that experience?
- Obviously obstacles can get in the way. What do you foresee as some of the key hurdles you'll be facing? How do you plan on tackling them?
- Your customers have a lot of choices. From your perspective, what do you believe is the core reason why they continue to do business with you versus others?
- Describe for me your long-term goals to grow the company.
- What are your biggest concerns for the future of your organization?
- What's the impact on you and your organization if you don't achieve the goals you shared with me?
- As you look back over the years with your company, what's the one takeaway lesson you'd like to share with others that could make a real difference in their careers?

A C-Suite Scenario

Here's an example of a salesperson calling on a C-suite executive, using some of the techniques we've discussed:

Alex works for Mugs 'n Stuff Promotional Products. He sells pens, coffee mugs, and T-shirts. Typically he calls on purchasing agents, buyers, sales managers, and product marketing managers. It's a price- and commodity-driven business.

Can Alex really call on a bank president? Yikes! Let's find out.

One of Alex's accounts is a local bank. It buys about ten thousand pens a year, which it gives away at local branches. During a recent visit with his contact—a purchasing agent for the bank—Alex learns that the bank is opening up five new branches in the community. There will be a big push to attract new customers.

"I have some ideas on how you can do that," Alex says. "It's not just about pens."

"Well, I'm not the guy to talk to," Alex's contact says. "But I do know that the president is all over this expansion. If you have good ideas, he's the one you'd want to talk to."

Alex prevails on his contact to make an introduction, and after several calls with the executive assistant, he manages to get a thirty-minute appointment with Bob, the bank president.

After the initial pleasantries, Alex says to Bob: "I've been working with a number of banks to create unique incentive programs to attract and retain good customers. To see if these programs might fit with your needs, may I ask you a few questions?"

Bob: Sure. Fire away.

Alex: I understand that you'll have five new branches opening up this year. Congratulations. So tell me, what's driving the growth and what are you hoping to accomplish over the next several years?

Bob: Our growth strategy is all about service. We take great pride in our ability to provide personalized service and get to know each customer, their goals and needs. We consider ourselves progressive in an industry that is slow to change. Our competition thinks that if they build a branch, customers will show up. We know it takes more than that.

We take a lot of pride in the fact that we build and sustain our relationships with customers. We go out to meet with them at their workplace and home and get active in promoting community projects. And we work hard to offer some of the best rates available nationally.

Our competition is basically happy with the status quo. They rely on customers' inertia. But they're not seeing how vulnerable they've become. We get at least two to three customers a day contacting us to switch their accounts over to us. So we know that customers aren't getting the service they expect from our competitors. That's why we want to get more aggressive in this regional market and start building more branches, five this year, and thirty more in the next several years.

Alex: That's exciting. So let's talk about the new branches opening up. How are you going to attract new customers?

Bob: We have an aggressive marketing plan for each branch, which includes advertising in the newspapers, radio, direct mail, and the Internet. Each branch manager has a goal. They're expected to sign up two hundred customers within the first six months of opening. It's a pretty aggressive plan but we have to achieve those types of numbers if we're going to continue to grow at least 15 percent per year.

Alex: Okay. Those are aggressive plans, but with advertising you'll stir up a lot of interest. So then what happens? Share with me what types of new-customer incentives and rewards programs you're considering, and how they align with your brand and reputation.

Bob: That's a good question. We'd be interested to hear your ideas. I can tell you, based on the demographic profile of our customers, that we're looking for high-value incentives such as gift cards, leather portfolios, maybe high-end softshell jackets or even customized tablets to motivate potential customers to sign up right away.

You mentioned our brand. It's something we really care about. We need to reinforce the message of who we are and our fifty years of being in business.

Alex: Fifty years says you've done a lot of things right to be where you are today. I definitely can provide you with some insight on what kinds of incentives work best. But before we go there, tell me about what an average new customer would be worth to you, and a little more about the demographic profile for the types of customers you're looking to draw in. . . .

So how is Alex doing?

You'll notice that he didn't pull out his laptop presentation or catalog and do a product dump of promotional items he could offer—even when he was invited to do so. Instead, he stayed focused on discovery and finding more about the needs, wants, and Bob's vision of the future.

As he continues to ask good questions, Alex learns that the average prospective bank customer is worth an average of $5,000 in deposits for basic checking and savings accounts. Add in auto and home loans and the value ranges from $30,000 to $500,000. It turns out that Bob will gladly invest $500 for each customer who signs up, especially if it's something that will set his bank apart from the competition. That's much more than Alex would have guessed, so he's glad he resisted the temptation to show Bob the lower-end incentives he'd originally been considering.

Alex sets up a follow-up meeting, where he presents some unique items that not only bring in business but reinforce the bank's brand. He walks away with an order for more than $200,000. Way to go, Alex!

25

Presentation Questions

How to Keep Buyers Awake, Engaged, and Wanting to Hear More

HAVE YOU EVER sat in a presentation where the salesperson just drones on and on—who they are, what they believe, how many years in business, a map showing their many locations, customers they've served, products they offer, features, benefits, blah, blah, blah? You're looking at the time and thinking about all of the things you need to do. Finally, the salesperson wraps up and says, "So, any questions?"

You think to yourself, "Please, no." You just want it to be over, and you hope nobody drags it out. So you quickly bring closure. "Great presentation," you say. "Very thorough. I have to run to another meeting. Let's touch base in a couple of weeks. You'll call me?"

Not every sales presentation is deadly. I've left some feeling energized and motivated to take action. But in my experience, that's the exception.

I've asked myself why. Why does a highly trained professional, whose number-one job is to communicate value, waste everyone's time, including his own?

I don't have a good answer, except to suggest that a good presentation is harder to pull off than it would appear. Salespeople often mistake manners for interest. You have the floor, and most people will sit quietly and listen out of politeness. We've been trained that way. In school, we're not allowed to walk out if the teacher is boring. If we go to a play or a movie, we're expected to sit through to the end. If we're invited to a meeting and the salesperson gives her spiel, we do the same thing. It doesn't mean we care.

I won't go into all the ways you can make presentations more effective. But if there's one thing you can do to keep them on track, relevant, and customer focused, it's to ask good questions. And that doesn't mean asking "Are there any questions?" at the end. In fact, if you're asking that, you might as well close your laptop and go home.

Asking questions as you go along turns the presentation around. It gets prospects engaged. It gets them to reveal what's important to them. It gets to the truth. A presentation shouldn't be a dog-and-pony show. It should be a dialogue. And the customer should be the star, not you.

Do Your Homework

To create a question-based presentation, start early.

The first order of business is to find out who's attending. And not just names and titles. You need to really understand who these people are and what motivates them.

Ask your contact: "So the president will be sitting in? Great. Tell me what you believe will be most important to her. What does she need to know? And the VP of operations will be there? What do you think he's looking for? What are his needs? And how about the HR director? What would she like to get out of the presentation? And why is that?"

If you don't know who will be at your meeting—what they care about or don't care about, what they expect, why they're investing their precious time in the meeting—how can you possibly create value?

Sometimes your contact can give you great insight because he has good relationships with these members. Other times, you're not so lucky. Your contact may not be willing to risk an opinion, or he may not have any insight beyond what the boss wants in his coffee. Even worse, sometimes he can lead you astray. Either he misread others' interests, or presents his own agenda as if it's his boss's.

When you ask about the other people and can't get a straight answer, it's a red flag that your contact is not in the "club" with these folks. But a presentation is too important to fly blind. You need to get the truth. Say to your contact: "I want to make sure I'm attentive to those who will be joining us. It's important that the presentation is meaningful and relevant to the issues everyone is facing. So I need their input. I need to reach out to Bob and Sue beforehand and have a brief conversation with them. What's the best way to reach them?

Or you might say: "Of the ten people who will be joining us, which two or three individuals would you recommend I reach out to beforehand to gain more insight into the issues the organization is facing?"

It would be rare for your contact to say, "I don't want you to talk to anyone else." In most cases, the contact will be thrilled that you'd take the extra time and effort to make your presentation successful. If they've set up a meeting and invited all these people, their reputation is on the line. The last thing they want is for you to show up unprepared and waste everyone's time.

In fact, if your contact *won't* give you that access, it's a huge red flag. What she's really saying is, "I don't value you. I don't trust you. I don't want to give you a leg up on your competitors (maybe the ones I really want to work with)."

In these situations you can often smell a rat. Someone wants to keep her existing vendor, but has been told to do her due diligence. She needs to cover her rear and get three bids. But she doesn't want you to succeed.

If you suspect that's what's going on, you have nothing to lose by standing your ground. I've been in situations where I've simply refused to make a presentation unless I can get the information I need. That creates a problem for the person who's using you for his own political purposes. It would be hard for him to explain to his bosses why you're backing out. Granted, you still have a steep hill to climb, but if you can engage the higher-ups and speak to their needs and interests, at least you have a fighting chance. Or you can continue to work on cultivating a relationship with your contact before you walk into a den of hungry wolves.

Going in Cold

In some cases, however, you simply don't have the time or opportunity to do your homework. You have to go in cold.

In that case, get to the presentation early so you have ample time to chat with people one-on-one. You only need a minute or two with each person to get a quick pulse and learn what's on their mind. Simply say, "Thanks for coming. So tell me one thing you'd like to take away from today's presentation." Or, "What prompted you to come to the meeting this morning?" Or, "What's one issue you're dealing with when it comes to . . . ?"

The information you gather allows you to adjust your presentation on the fly to make it more relevant. I'll often take comments from three or four participants and use that feedback to open up the session. For example, I might say, "Good morning. My name is Paul Cherry. Thanks for joining us today. I understand some of the key issues you're facing are these . . ."

And then I'll list them on a whiteboard. For example:

1. How to motivate your team to do more with limited resources
2. How to prospect for new business, versus calling on the same old customers
3. How to protect your hard-earned margins against price erosion

Then I'll continue: "So am I correct that these are your issues? Are there other issues we could add to these? How should we prioritize them?"

This is a very effective opening. It sets the stage for a question-and-answer dialogue and immediately engages the participants. It puts you in the role of facilitator rather than presenter. You've hit key pain points and quickly demonstrated that you're a good listener.

But, you may ask, what about my slides? Time is short. I've got a lot to cover. And I worked so hard on them!

Remember that buyers care a lot more about their issues than about your slides. I've seen instances where the dialogue is so powerful that the salesperson never gets to the deck at all—and still wins the business! Don't rush your customer. Set the stage, tap into peoples' emotions to get them excited about being there. Then they'll want to hear everything you have to tell them.

As you go through your presentation, use questions liberally. Spend two or three minutes on a key point—maybe five minutes at the most. Then stop—and pose a question. For example: "How does what I've shared with you so far relate to what you're experiencing?"

Don't feel that you have to present the question to the whole group. You can focus on one or two individuals. But don't let any one person steal the show. As a presenter and facilitator, you have to manage the conversation. Draw out the people who are quiet. Give everyone a say.

Use questions throughout the presentation to keep it on track. The questions can be very simple: "Does this make sense?" "Is this relevant?" "We hear _____ from other clients. How's that compare to what you're facing?" "Based on what I just shared with you on this slide, how would

____ be of value to you? What would it enable you to do that you're not doing now?"

Sometimes you can ask rhetorical questions—where you're not asking for a response but just want the group to think. For example: "Have you ever wondered why some salespeople with a lot of experience and knowledge are sometimes the worst performers? I raise this question because many of my clients share this concern. Now let me share with you some of the reasons. . . . "

Or you can raise a question that surfaces an emotion you know they are currently experiencing on the job. For example: "Have you ever had one of those days where you're putting out a lot of fires, responding to one request after another, and it's now at the end of the week, you're looking at the stack of paperwork and emails that you still have to respond to and wonder, when's it gonna ever end? Anybody here have that experience? Well, I hope to provide some answers...."

If your audience isn't engaging with you, put out a question you typically hear from your existing clients and prospects. For example: "One question we often hear is, 'How do I get started?'" Or, "Clients often raise their hands at this point and ask, 'How do I show the ROI?'"

Every presentation is different, of course, but you get the general idea. Good questions turn a one-sided show into a give-and-take. The answers can take you in surprising directions, but they keep you focused on what matters to the buyers. They make everyone a participant. And if people are involved in creating the solution, they're far more likely to buy it.

Index

223